JASON VANCLEF

The
WEALTH CODE

D1736389

HOW THE RICH STAY RICH IN GOOD TIMES AND BAD.

For Tami and Grant. Your patience and understanding while your husband/father was writing this book will always be greatly appreciated. Here's to spending more time at the park.

Jason/Dad

Acknowledgments

A few people are directly responsible for bringing this book to reality. First, Nancy Vanclef, my mom, who had a huge impact on editing this book and smoothing out the rough edges. Your contributions and ideas sorted out my 2:00 AM feverish writings and made them coherent. You were the perfect sounding board. To my dad, Herve Vanclef, for making my mom's life easier during her editing of this book and providing me with a viewpoint that you can accomplish twelve different projects all at the same time. To my brother Cristian, from afar, you've always demonstrated to me that genius doesn't have to come from a book but from so many other attributes in life. Dail Hutchinson, my grandfather, who was the inspiration for my entire career as a financial advisor.

I also want to recognize Mike Janis, who contributed to many of the real estate and oil/gas sections, pulling together numerous question/answer topics to further educate our clients on complex issues. Your diligence and attention to detail eased some of the more difficult sections of this book for me to write.

Lastly, I want to thank all my clients who have constantly inspired me to grow and adapt in this ever-changing economic landscape. This book is dedicated to you.

―――

Preface

A frog if placed into a pot of boiling water will jump out and save itself. If that same frog is placed in the pot with cold water and heat is slowly applied, it will boil itself to death.

Running a financial firm in Santa Monica, CA, we meet hundreds of people each year and discuss their finances. Nothing cuts more to the core than people and their money. With each passing year, and seeing the faces of hard working people who have had their retirement goals shattered time and time again by the stock markets, I question, "Is the stock market just a big pot of water with the heat slowly being turned on?"

I feel that if this book were written in 2006, most people would disregard it. "The stock markets are great," they would say, "It has made us a lot of money." Though we had experienced a terrible correction between 2000 and 2002, and even though in 2006 most people were nowhere close to their account values before that market crash, the sense that all was right and their money was coming back was the prevailing belief. Even though the heat was being applied to the water pot, most people stayed the course.

I hope the timing for this book, during the eye of the financial hurricane we are currently experiencing and after the horrendous loss of wealth we just suffered with the market crash between 2007–2009, will give people a new perspective and control over their finances, for which many are currently searching. Most people are now beginning to realize that maybe the water pot is not the best place for their money, and the revolt against staying the course has begun.

Jason Vanclef

May 1, 2009

Contents

Introduction

If what you thought to be true turned out NOT to be true, when would you want to know?

Imagine you are on a gurney and they are wheeling you into surgery. You were out hiking in the woods, got caught in a freak snowstorm, and ended up with frostbite on your left big toe. In order to save your left foot, they have to amputate the left big toe.

Under the intense lights, as they are about knock you out with the gas, you happen to look over and see the instruction sheet to the surgeons for this operation. Much to your horror, someone has mistakenly written incorrect instructions. They read, "Amputate the RIGHT foot."

The doctors are just about to knock you out. Would you agree you are at a juncture in your life?

What do you do? Do you scream bloody murder or rationalize to yourself, *No, these doctors are smart; they would never cut off the wrong foot. They know what they are doing.* Do you go to sleep hoping for the best?

Hopefully, you choose the option to scream bloody murder. If you choose "hope for the best" and wake up after surgery with your right foot gone, it will only add insult to injury, since they still have to amputate the left big toe.

To relate to this story, think back to March of 2000. Most people's stock market investments had gone up five years in a row, and they felt their financial advisor was a genius. Then they noticed their statements in April, and again in May and June. The money they had was disappearing. Instead of most people screaming bloody murder, they rationalized to themselves that their advisors were smart, that they knew what they were doing. Most people put on the gas mask, went to sleep, and hoped for the best.

To their shock, many people awoke in October of 2002 with their portfolios down 50–80%. Not only had the doctors amputated the right foot, but they had taken the whole leg, both arms, and an ear.

Look what happened between January 2008 and February 2009. The previous five years of market gains were wiped out, and the markets collapsed to 1997 levels. Once again, we went to sleep and awoke to find numerous body parts amputated. At this pace, we might as well start looking into bionics.

Why is it that with money we humans tend to throw common sense out the window with complex rationalizations? We second-guess what should be done with simple axioms such as "buy and hold," or "dollar cost average." "Don't worry about the long-term; your portfolio will come back." This sounds good, unless you're already nearing retirement.

Here's another story to relate to our silliness:

One sunny day, you are driving to the beach, when all of a sudden your car makes a loud clunk. As you slow down to see what has happened, you notice your car shifting between gears erratically, and you suspect your clutch has bought the farm. Good thing for you it is a Tuesday and you are playing hooky from work. The bad thing is now it will be spent at the auto mechanic's versus on a beautiful, warm beach.

After the mechanic gives you a quote for one thousand dollars to repair your clutch, you give a sigh of defeat and grab a sandwich and a movie as your car is being fixed. The day off from work isn't completely wasted.

A few hours later, you pick up your car and begrudgingly pay the thousand dollars. You jump in and start to drive off. Lo and behold, your car is still shifting erratically and making the same loud clunking sound.

What is the first thing you do? You turn around immediately, clunk your way back to the mechanic, and demand they fix it or give you back your money.

After taking your car back, the mechanic looks at it again and then advises you to keep driving it for a while. It will fix itself over time. What is your reaction to this advice? "You're nuts! My car can't fix itself. If I keep driving around like this, the damage will get worse, and I'll be out of pocket even more money." At this point, you fire the mechanic and take your clunky car to another mechanic who can fix the clutch.

How many of us are driving broken portfolios, nest eggs that seem to be going nowhere? When you go to your financial advisor, what do they tell you? "Don't worry; you're buy and hold. Keep driving that broken portfolio, and it will fix itself."

How many broken cars fix themselves? The same goes for money. Wall Street wants you to believe that stocks always go up. They want you to stay in their fee generating investments for many more years, hoping for your portfolio to fix itself. Sometimes, your portfolio does seem like it is on the mend. The clunking sound goes away for a while. For instance, many people who lost big between 2000 and 2002 made back a lot of their losses from 2003 to 2007. But, like a broken clutch that really doesn't fix itself, although the clunking sound went away for a bit, a bigger problem was brewing under the hood, something much worse.

As you were driving down the financial freeway in 2008 and the beginning of 2009, not only did your clutch freeze up again, but now, the whole transmission fell out and snapped the rear axle to boot. That thousand-dollar clutch seems cheap now.

Money is an odd creature. Some people can spend all day possessed by it, others spend their days avoiding the very thought of it, and most of us are somewhere in between. It ruins relationships, creates green-eyed monsters, and generally frustrates most everyone who tries to deal with it. Strangely, some of the brightest and best educated can become bumbling fools when it comes to protecting and growing their wealth.

The eternal question is, "What is the best way to grow my wealth?" The answers you receive tend to reflect the viewpoint of the person giving the advice: a Wall Street hot shot, a real estate guru, a gold bug, a lotto winner, or an entrepreneur.

As with anything that is important to us, we try to hire people who are better at a specific job than we are. When I get sick, I see a doctor. When I want to redo my front yard, I hire a landscape architect. And, of course, when I want to grow my wealth, I hire a qualified financial advisor.

The problem with wealth of course is that there is no holy grail for protecting and growing it. If you ask ten financial advisors how to protect and grow your nest egg, you will probably get ten different answers. Although the answers will be different, there generally is a common thread. It usually revolves around using Wall Street as the key to increasing and protecting your wealth.

In writing this book, I hope to show that Wall Street isn't the key, but a single player on a team of all stars that when working together as a team has a much better chance of reaching your financial goals.

Contrary to popular belief, most people who invest only with Wall Street see their wealth decline far more often than it propels them toward their goals. How often do you read about people who invested in the markets for thirty years, only to watch half of it disappear right before retirement due to declining stock markets? These stories are far too numerous to count.

Most who are reading this book are thinking, "Hog wash, the stock market is great for building long-term wealth." I challenge the reader to think about their money in the stock market. When carefully analyzed and totaled, did the majority of the investment balance come from market gains alone, or did the act of saving and adding hard earned dollars each year cause the principal to increase? The answer to this question is very important.

For most people, the majority of their wealth comes from tangible investments. Their real estate holdings, a business built from the ground up, a product they created and sold, oil and gas royalties, and so on. More often than not, the money they have in the stock market is the excess from these other more lucrative endeavors.

The title of this book, *The Wealth Code: How to Rich Stay Rich in Good Times and Bad*, is meant to elicit different questions, such as:

What is conventional thinking in terms of finance, and how is it holding back my wealth building process?

Are other people using financial ideas and strategies of which I am not aware?

Is there a code for wealth, a map that we can follow to provide a more secure road to or in retirement?

I believe these questions will be answered in the following chapters.

———

Chapter 1
Freeing Your Estate from Conventional Thinking

Here's an example of conventional thinking. Talking head after talking head preaches pay off your mortgage with extra payments. You'll save tens of thousands of dollars and will own your home outright sooner.

What are you doing by paying extra into the home? You are creating a situation that the mortgage holder salivates for. Each time you pay extra, you place more money in their hands for them to invest for THEIR well-being, and also you lower THEIR risk. Let me repeat again. As you put more equity into the home, the mortgage gets smaller, and there is more equity protecting the lien holder in case you can't make your mortgage payment for whatever reason. Death, disability, and divorce are common unforeseen reasons. If their risk is lowering, what is happening to your risk? It is going up. You have more to lose if you can't pay your mortgage, and they take your home to auction and only cover what is owed to them, the mortgage balance. Auctions are not meant to protect the seller; they are meant to protect the lien holders.

Here is what I call unconventional or uncommon knowledge. Instead of paying extra into your home, make the exact same payment into a side account. Something that can earn 5–6% each year and compound on itself, and is fairly liquid. Even something with surrender charges will work. In the same time you would have paid off your house, in actuality faster, the side account will have grown to equal your remaining mortgage balance. At that point, you can take your side account and pay off your mortgage all at one time and own your home outright. I'll explain ways to earn the 5–6% in Chapter 7, but for now, assume you can easily achieve those results.

The advantage to this financial strategy is many fold.

First, you have an emergency reserve of immediate cash. Is equity in your home more liquid than a side account? No way. Unless you have a line of credit already established and it hasn't been taken away, like so many are today in early 2009, then your equity in your home is stuck. Without a pre-existing line of credit, you could apply for a line of credit, refinance your mortgage, or sell your home to unlock the equity to pay for your emergency. Today, all three choices are exceptionally difficult and time consuming. In an emergency, time is not a luxury we usually have.

Second, by not paying down your mortgage, you will retain more mortgage interest to deduct, which will give you greater tax rebates from Uncle Sam. If you really wanted to be aggressive with your saving, take the rebate generated due to the interest deduction and apply it toward your side account.

The point of my example is this: Many ideas are spread that sound good on the surface, but when you dive in and uncover the true logic of a situation, many times, the right answer is very different or is the exact opposite. Conventional thinking in finance has caused a lot of pain and hardship for people, and it has usually been promoted by the groups that have a vested interest in staying the course.

———

Chapter 2
The Best Portfolios Are Mixtures of Many Different Asset Classes

Take for instance the word "diversification." You may have been told that if you have lots of stocks, bonds, and mutual funds, you are diversified. In actuality, your portfolio has a lot of only one asset class. **There are many asset classes to invest in, and the best portfolios are mixtures of many different asset classes.**

Basketball is a great way to demonstrate the concept of a True Asset Class diversified portfolio.

Does it seem a bit unfair that in the Olympics the USA basketball team has the best players from the NBA all working together? By cherry picking the superstars from each team—knowing their statistics, their abilities, and track records—and crafting them together to make a super team, Team USA fields the most competitive team available.

I was watching a game between USA and the Canada in the 2007 Summer Olympics; the final score was 113 to 63. Pretty close compared to other matches the USA team had already played. Watching the game, players would go in and out. At one point Kobe Bryant, the superstar from the LA Lakers, took a five-minute break. Lo and behold, the score became more and more imbalanced, even though one of the greatest players in the NBA was not on the court. Why? Because Lebron James, Dwight Howard, Jason Kidd, and others were still playing, and each was a superstar in his own right. I would argue that if Kobe Bryant had broken his leg in this game, Lebron and the rest of the guys would still have won and eventually would still have captured the gold medal.

If Kobe broke his leg during the regular season with the Lakers, it would have a devastating outcome for his team. Kobe is the all-star of his team, but on the Olympic team, he is one of many all-stars. The Olympic team would have a minor setback, at best.

The difference in skill between the Lakers and the all-star Olympic team is the same as the difference between a portfolio that got crushed in 2008 and one which survived the storm and actually grew because of true diversification.

This is the philosophy of our group. We have built our own team of financial all-stars, who excel in many areas of wealth building through true asset class diversification.

Diversification is a word that means different things to different people. It is supposed to make people feel better about their investments, that they are doing the right thing. The problem is the viewpoint of the person promoting the idea. As previously discussed, most financial advisors view the world in two colors: stocks and bonds.

I will proceed to show you one prevalent view of diversification and then my own view. One viewpoint of the financial world looks like the teeter-totter below:

Typical financial planner's view of the investment universe

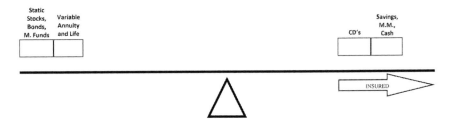

This example of diversification includes stocks, bonds, mutual funds, variable annuities, and CDs, which I jokingly call Certificates of Depreciation or Disappointment. More on that later.

If I were a carpenter and I had a business building one-legged dining room tables, it's easy to imagine that these tables would fall over due to instability at the slightest push, and my business wouldn't last very long. No one would be silly enough to buy a one-legged table because ultimately it would not do the job as intended—to provide a stable platform for eating.

Stocks, bonds, mutual funds, and variable annuities represent essentially one asset class, or one leg of a multi-leg financial table. The other legs are asset classes that are independent of the stock market. Examples include real estate, oil/gas programs, collateralized notes, equipment leases, rare coins, and fixed annuities, to name a few. These are called non-correlated investments.

The problem with Wall Street's single leg viewpoint is that no matter how many parts of this one leg you put together, you still have only one leg on your financial table. If that leg fails, your table will come crashing down.

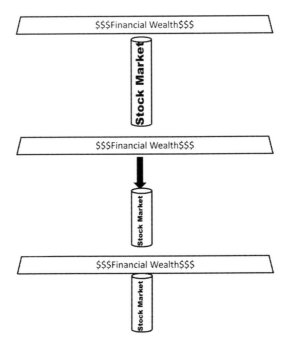

Wall Street can be compared to the carpenter building unstable one-legged tables, although this narrow approach is all that most groups offer the majority of investors. There are several reasons why the vast majority of investors invest all their hard earned money in one legged tables: It's all they know, it's all their advisors know, and these are the opportunities all the large firms, holding their money, will provide for them to invest in.

If you go to the grocery story very hungry and the store only has apples and oranges for sale, guess what? You are going to buy apples and oranges. You don't have any other choice, since you choose to shop at a grocery store with limited options. That is Wall Street's version of "diversification," a one-legged table built of stocks, bonds, mutual funds, and variable annuities. Although variable annuities do represent another leg on the table, the foundation for variable annuities is still the stock market and thus is essentially the same leg.

———

Chapter 3
The Key to Protecting and Building Wealth in Good Times and Bad

We strive to build an Olympic-quality team for our clients using the best-of-class investment ideas and offering a financial table with numerous legs. Just as the Olympic basketball team includes the best players from the NBA, we believe finding the best players in each asset class is imperative to long-term financial success. Though in any given year one of the legs on a truly diversified financial table might fail, as long as you have many other legs on the table to provide support, you will survive whatever financial storm comes your way.

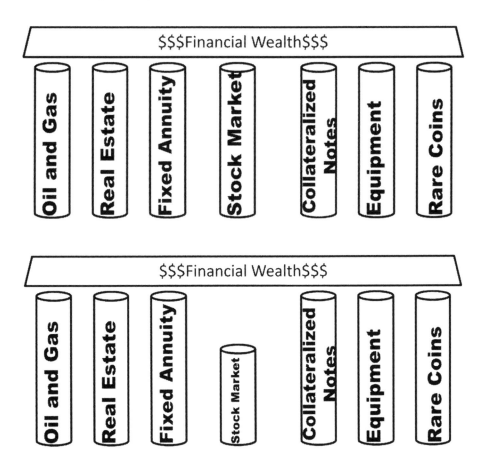

It is the philosophy my firm uses to build a client's portfolio, and it is why we threw one hell of a client appreciation event on November 16, 2008, inviting over two hundred fifty of our most established clients and their friends to a gathering where they could all sit around and talk. I started off the night with a simple speech.

"Do you think Wall Street is inviting their top clients to a party in this brutal year and encouraging them to all talk to each other and compare notes? I don't think so."

Why did we do that? Because, except for a few people in the room, all of their portfolios were net positive. What is net positive? When adding all the legs of their Asset Class Diversified Table together, including dividends and growth, though some legs had shrunken a bit, the other legs of their financial table grew and overcame the losses of the bad legs. And thus, overall, their financial tables grew.

The few people in the room who lost money in 2008 were the ones who chose to work with us only on stock market investments. They chose for us to build an improved one-legged table for them, in spite of our recommendations to spread their funds into a combination of other legs to provide balance.

The good news for them: the improved stock market leg fell 8.6% in 2008. Much better than the 38.5% the SP500 fell.

Asset Class Diversification

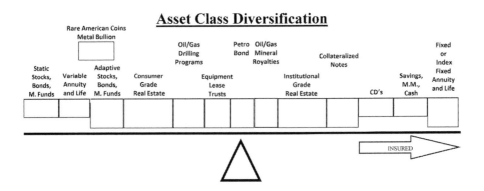

The above table shows all the investments on the planet. Everything can be grouped into these basic categories. You will find a more complete discussion of each investment class in Chapter 7.

As of this writing, I just turned thirty-eight. Some people would say I am too young to know anything. Yet how many of those same people threw a client appreciation event for their clients in 2008? More likely, how many of them went into hiding and gave the same old excuses for their clients' losses of 20–40% or more? The proof is in the pudding, as they say.

Ask yourself a question. What happened to your portfolio during 2008, and what did your advisor tell you were the reasons?

Though young and not having twenty years in the business, I know one simple fact. I can never be the best at everything. There will always be somebody better. Knowing this provides clarity and vision.

If I can't be the best, who is?

Who has the track record, the years of experience, and the know-how to do the job they say they are going to do? What groups in each asset class have demonstrated that they are the best or one of the best? These are the specialists whom we hire on behalf of our clients.

Our job for clients, as their financial advisor, is to be a general practitioner. Someone who spends his time reading everything he can get his hands on, in many disciplines of finance. Not just stocks and bonds, but insurance, estate planning, real estate, oil/gas, pensions, mortgages, rare coins, and so forth. Being well versed but always hungry for more. Never satisfied with what we have learned, but constantly trying to improve as well as question what we believe to be true.

Isn't that why the person with a BMW or Ford hires an experienced mechanic who specializes in BMWs or Fords? I don't believe any one person can call himself a financial advisor and try to be an expert at all these different jobs. The stock picker, the real estate buyer, the developmental oil/gas driller, the coin collector: each requires considerable expertise. We choose to hire those who focus on one thing and one thing only, and we put them together as your Olympic team.

As an example, many of the groups we hire in the Institutional Grade Real Estate asset class have been in business longer than I've been alive. They have focused only on this asset class their entire careers, and they don't deviate from their basic game plans. They are among the best of this asset class.

We do not hire them to provide services for other legs of the financial table, as we don't hire a BMW mechanic to fix a Ford truck.

When looking for a financial advisor, ask them what legs of the financial table they work with, and more importantly will not work with, and why?

If they tell you a particular investment asset class is terrible, high risk, and will lose you all your money, ask them to give specific examples and experiences. No generalities. We find time and again that financial advisors who know nothing about a particular investment, or cannot represent a particular investment because their broker dealer (employer) forbids them from offering it, will automatically represent it as too high of risk. Or they will claim that they are "conservative," meaning careful with the investments they recommend. It's bad, terrible; stay away. Then they promptly follow up with, "I have a great mutual fund, stock, bond, blah, blah, blah." Think about it. If someone were truly conservative in their approach, would they allow their clients to lose 30–40% or more of their wealth while holding stocks and bonds they have recommended?

Up to this point, we have covered the concept of conventional thinking and how it is not always in your best interest but possibly somebody else's. Our view of most financial advisors is that most are very myopic in their ability to help people with their finances and with the concept of true asset class diversification as a means to protect and grow an estate, in the best and worst of times.

Chapter 4 introduces the concept of your wealth bucket and the process of building wealth. It covers why certain firms focus only on high net worth clients, as well as common brokerisms, a word I use to describe the excuses a financial advisor will use to never admit a mistake. Chapter 4 also discusses a simple secret of the wealthiest people in the world.

Chapter 5 describes the common leaks in your wealth bucket, leaks from which countless dollars drain out of your pockets and into others every year.

Chapter 6 dives much deeper into the concept of True Asset Class Diversification and gives a viewpoint on money that even a third grader can grasp, yet few financial advisors ever will. This chapter also begins laying out a road map for making changes that will greatly improve the strength and stability of your financial table.

Chapter 7 covers all of the investment asset classes and goes into the pros and cons of each one. There is no such thing as the perfect investment, something that returns double-digit growth every year, is guaranteed, and is completely liquid. All investments have their drawbacks. The idea is to find those investments whose pitfalls are not bad for your situation and to blend them together with many different financial tools, which will provide investment balance.

Chapter 8 will provide a framework for you, the reader, to understand and craft a successful financial plan for yourself. You are not expected to be able to implement a complete financial plan, considering most of the investments we'll introduce have to be purchased through a licensed financial advisor or broker, but nonetheless, you'll be able to put together the blueprint that will match your goals, and not the planner's pocket book. In this chapter, as well as Appendix A, there will be case studies of plans we've implemented for clients that have successfully withstood the ravages of the 2007–2009 recession.

Chapter 9 covers a brief overview of our thoughts on where life insurance and annuities have a place in one's portfolio.

I believe that, once finished with this short book, you will have the tools to build a strong financial table for yourself and your family, and be better able to ride out the worst of any economic calamity that comes your way.

———

Chapter 4
The Process of Wealth

Why do some people have a knack for making money? There will always be a part that is a god-given talent, such as ambition and self-discipline, but for most who become wealthy, many of them had great mentors and guides along the way. Why reinvent the wheel when you can get a head start from someone who has been there and done that?

The process of building wealth is the ability to accumulate and protect one's wealth. It is understanding the fundamental steps that will take you down the financial road toward your goals, versus causing you to take a detour. Basics such as consuming less than you produce and saving the difference is just one building block in a pyramid of concepts that serve to move you in the right direction.

I've always felt education is the most important block in one's foundation. The constant desire to improve your understanding of the world by reading what others have to say is crucial. More important than what you read on any given topic is just that you do read. You have demonstrated this basic principle by reading this book. You might not agree with everything I say, but if you can pull out a few good ideas, then your time and money were worth it.

Clients always ask me for book recommendations, and I usually say if someone spent the time to write something and goes through the effort to publish it, then there has to be a few good ideas in any book. Just read.

My goal in the following chapters is to define the process of building and preserving wealth as it relates to financial planning and investments in general. Too often, people are stuck in a rut because they don't know what they don't know.

They are invested in mutual funds because that is all that has been presented to them or all that they know. They don't realize that there are many other opportunities that are appropriate for their circumstances, which they should investigate and from which they could prosper.

At our firm, education is priority number one. We are here to teach people who walk in our door as much or as little as they are willing to learn.

We never charge or request retainers. Education is always free. Why do we do this? We need to be paid, right? Of course, but from the client's perspective, most financial advisors work hurriedly to make the sale and then move on. Many people are disillusioned with the idea of working with a financial advisor because most have been burned by the process that Wall Street promotes: the quick sale.

An interesting question sums up most advisors out there.

"Would you rather have Tiger Woods' golf clubs or Tiger Woods' golf swing?"

If I had Tiger Woods' clubs and he had a three-foot, two-by-four piece of wood, he would take my lunch money hands down.

It is his billion-dollar swing that wins all the money. A billion is the estimate of what he will be worth by the time he turns thirty-five. Not bad for playing a game with a stick and a ball.

When you see firms with high net worth minimums, it doesn't mean you are getting a better, more educated experience. It just means they don't want to waste time on small fries because they are more interested in selling golf clubs as fast as possible and moving on to the next prospect.

The critical part of financial planning should be education. Learning how to swing the club. In my opinion, groups that cloak their activities in the most secrecy and fastest transaction times are the ones with the least to offer or are really scams, like the Madoff or Stanford Ponzi schemes—the "just trust us" attitude. Another fundamental block to building wealth should always be a healthy dose of skepticism.

I am not a follower of the cliché, "If it sounds too good to be true, it probably is," because many of the great investments out there do sound almost too good to be true. With a lot of due diligence and education, you realize they are not too good to be true, but they are just uncommon because few representatives are able to offer them. If you were to presume that few representatives offer them because they are bad investments, you would assume wrong. Many great, uncommon investments are highly conservative in their design, and with time, they generate great returns and tax benefits. They are uncommon because the commission schedule they pay to the representative is too low for most firms to want to offer them.

Wealth Bucket 101

Let's begin with a visual concept we'll use for the rest of the book. I like to describe wealth using the metaphor of a large wooden bucket. It is a sturdy bucket with a good handle and steel ribbons encircling the tub. However, the bucket is made from wood and because it is not indestructible; it is prone to springing leaks. These leaks are the source of most of the frustration people experience with their money. The leaks occur because of everything from high taxes due to poor tax planning, excessive investment fees, and insufficient estate planning, to limited investment diversification and withdrawing too much money from a nest egg as currently designed. Chapter 5 goes into great detail about the leaks in the bucket.

In the introduction, we made it pretty clear that we believe in using many investment tools other than the stock market. Several leaks are directly related to Wall Street and the motivation to move money from our pockets into theirs, for their own well-being.

Other leaks in the bucket are due to not understanding the process of building and preserving wealth. For instance, buying liabilities with cash represents a huge leak in the bucket. We are told to never have debt, to pay for everything with cash and you'll be bullet proof. Yes, paying for everything with cash is stress free and a safe route to take but not very good for building wealth, especially when purchasing an item that will depreciate over time. An automobile is a perfect example of something that should not be paid for with cash.

Most people who have a large net worth realize the importance of using other people's money to add zeros to their bottom line.

What is a liability? **Anything you buy that takes money from your pocket at the end of the day.** A personal residence is a liability. Conventional thinking says a house is a great investment. Actually, it takes money out of your bucket every year for mortgage costs, property taxes, insurance, and repairs. The saying goes, better to buy than rent. Not necessarily. If you had bought a $584,000 median valued home in Los Angeles in 2006, that house as of April 2009 would be worth about $319,000. In a mere two and a half years, the resale value would have dropped $265,000. Had you stayed in an apartment and paid rent of $2,500 per month, you would have spent only $75,000. In terms of net worth, you would be almost $190,000 ahead of the homebuyer.

Of course, there are numerous reasons to own your home, from personal enjoyment to pride of ownership, but financially speaking, it is not always a black and white decision.

The opposite of a liability is, of course, an asset. **Assets are investments that put money in your pocket at the end of the day.**

If people focused on using their wealth to buy assets, they would keep themselves out of so much financial trouble. Many who bought real estate between 2004 and 2007 bought a liability-type property, hoping it would appreciate. They now find themselves on the wrong side of a mortgage payment and upside down on the property. Buying for appreciation and not for positive cash flow has them in a financial bind.

Had they bought an asset property that generated positive cash flow each month, they wouldn't need to worry so much about the value of the property falling because they have time on their side. Worst case, they can buy time by collecting rent checks until the dirt eventually becomes more valuable.

Unlike the stock market, where time isn't necessarily the panacea for bad investments, we can agree that with enough time dirt will eventually inflate upwards, unless the property has other really serious flaws.

Another example of a liability that people buy for cash is an automobile. We enjoy our cars, and we need them, unless one lives in New York City or San Francisco, where there is great public transportation. At the end of the day, most cars lose value and end up costing money. They are a convenience, not an appreciating asset.

In summary, your wealth will grow as you buy investments that will appreciate over time and not depreciate. It is a key to the wealth-building process and to expanding your bucket of wealth.

Buy Assets to Pay For Liabilities!
Basically, how can I buy an asset that generates a positive cash flow to pay for a depreciating asset (a liability) that I desire?

For example, you see a beautiful Lexus in the window of a showroom. The cost is fifty thousand dollars. This is your dream car, and you've got the money to pay for it in cash. Sounds like common, conventional thinking, doesn't it? But, you should ask yourself a question: "Where can I put fifty thousand dollars to earn enough positive cash flow to make the monthly payments on a multi-year car purchase loan?"

Using the principle of using other people's money, you begin to search for multi-unit small apartment buildings around the country. You find an eight-unit building in a small city in Tennessee for two hundred thousand dollars, and after running the numbers, the net cash flow for this building with a fifty thousand dollar down payment is around seven hundred dollars per month.

Sounds like a lot of work to buy your dream car, right? It is much easier to pull out the checkbook, whip out a check for fifty thousand dollars, and sail down the road that afternoon with your hair flapping in the wind.

What have you accomplished with this quick purchase? As soon as you drove off the car lot, you lost ten thousand dollars from your bucket of wealth due to depreciation on the car. After a few years, the car is only worth twenty-five thousand dollars from continued depreciation. Another fifteen thousand dollars is lost from your bucket of wealth.

The person who spent time and effort to buy the little building in Tennessee now has seven hundred dollars per month in cash flow from their eight-unit building to cover the car payment on a six-year loan for the Lexus.

The apartment rents won't cover all the expenses of the car for the first year or so, but the beauty of an apartment building is you can raise the rents year after year. Maybe by the third year, your net cash flow from the property is one thousand dollars per month, and you are now able to cover the expenses of the car, with some extra to pay for gas. By the time the six years are up and your Lexus is paid off, the little building you bought in Tennessee is likely worth the same as you paid for it, if not more, and you still have at least the twelve thousand dollars in positive cash flow for rent coming in each year. The value of the Lexus, on the other hand, is much lower than its original cost. Note the comparisons below.

Net result after six years:
Impulse buy of the Lexus with cash:

Car	Year 6 estimated value: $10,000
Cash Flow	Negative each year for gas, insurance, and repairs
Lost wealth from the bucket	At least the $50,000 purchase price

Buy the Asset (eight-unit apartment building) to pay for the liability (Lexus):

Car	Year 6 estimated value: $10,000
Cash flow	Positive by at least $12,000 per year
Wealth preserved	$50,000 down payment
Wealth gained	Equity build up in property
Tax Benefits	Mortgage and depreciation deductions against income. More money in your pocket!

The added benefit of taking the road less traveled to purchase the dream car is that after the six years, you could use the positive cash flow received from the apartment building to buy another dream car and renew the hair flapping and smiles of the open road.

What does the person who bought the car outright have to show for it after six years? A beat up Lexus worth about ten thousand dollars and lost wealth and opportunity, at the cost of tens of thousands of dollars.

So much for conventional thinking!

Fortune 400 Secret

What do the four hundred wealthiest people in the world know about wealth building? That it doesn't come from the stock market. If you look at the composition of the Fortune 400, their wealth has come from tangible investments: real estate, oil/gas, timber, built a business, or the good old American non-tangible way: they inherited it. Only one guy on the list truly made it from the stock market, Warren Buffet. Now, I know some will argue that there are a few hedge fund managers who made their money from the stock market, but I would respond that they made their money from the fees they charged their clients within the business of a hedge fund.

Your response might be, well of course, they had great returns in the stock market for their clients and received due compensation.

Hedge funds are the biggest rich person scam going. The allure is the exclusivity, almost country club feel, for investors with high account minimums, and the positive spin with which they promote performance fees. Performance fees are the fees paid for those returns a hedge fund makes over and above a common market benchmark. Typically, the hedge fund takes 20–25% of the excess profits. The nature of these fees is they are measured quarterly, thus making them a sucker's bet for the client and the ultimate Vegas casino for the manager.

The manager is basically swinging for the fences each quarter, and if he or she hits it out of the park one time from sheer luck, the excess above the benchmark is usually enough for the manager to retire many lifetimes over. For example, in 2006, Amaranth Advisors effectively lost 65% of their clients' money in one month, between August and September, yet the lead manager for the fund had hit homeruns the previous quarters and made almost $100 million for himself that year. Not bad for bankrupting his clients. Another example would be T. Boone Pickens, the famous oil/gas hedge fund manager. T. Boone made over $2 billion of income in 2007 and lost 97% of his clients' money in 2008.

When a fund manager comes to our office to tout their excellent performance, I ask two simple questions:

1. What is your ten-year average?
2. How much leverage do you use?

The reason for the first question is history. Don't show me one, three, or even five years of performance. Show me at least ten years. That way, I know they will have seen some bad years, and I can gauge their ability to protect the principal. The second question tells me the real returns of the group. For instance, if the answer to question one is 10% and question two is answered as 3:1 leverage, all we need to do is divide the 10% by three to equal a real return minus leverage, or 3.33%. Most CDs pay that much without the risk.

We believe in only using managers who use all cash. Without the crutch of high leverage in the good times, they really have to perform well. In the bad times, the benefit of not using leverage is very apparent. These accounts tend to have much lower volatility or price swings, and fewer of our clients are biting their nails down to the bone.

Brokerisms
Part of the process of wealth building is understanding when you are hearing a lot of baloney, and more importantly, being realistic with your finances. Being able to make changes by addressing investments that are underperforming will serve you well. Wall Street is artful at changing

perceptions to make their mistakes look like opportunities so that you will remain invested with them for as long as possible. You may have heard the running joke, "What do you call the advisor who keeps his clients in accounts, even though they have lost 20–50%? Vice President!"

Every year, millions are spent on marketing campaigns using mumbo jumbo to grab your attention and grab your money. Part of the campaign is to change perceptions of reality. I'm sure most of you have heard the common brokerisms, or excuses, used to never admit a mistake and give them an opportunity to sell you something else.

"Don't worry, you're a long-term investor; you're buy and hold!"

If you would have had to hold stocks between 1881 and 1921 before you made any money, would forty years count as long-term? What about 1929 to 1954, or another famous bear market, 1965 to 1982? I take a very basic view of bear markets. If the stock market revisits a point on the journey, then the current sideways bear market started at the first point. For instance, in early March 2009, we touched levels on the S&P500 not seen since 1997. Thus, for most people, their money had gone sideways for twelve years.

Most would argue that the current bear market started in 2000. Again, I take a simple approach to money. If I had a one hundred dollars in 1997, and today in 2009, I have only one hundred dollars, my money hasn't grown one penny, and that is a bear market for me. There will always be scientific methodologies to identify when an official recession or bear market began, but again, for most people, they just care that their investments are worth more than in the past.

"It's cheaper at this price; we should dollar cost average!"

Imagine you are on the Titanic and you're sailing on the Atlantic at night. Suddenly, the ship rocks violently and lists to the starboard. You ask the captain what happened, and the captain answers, "Don't be afraid; this is a strong ship. Instead of panicking and selling like other people, why don't we take advantage of the cheap prices for a cabin suite, spend more money on better accommodations, and ride it out."

Do you want to listen to that captain or to Captain B who says, "I will admit that I don't know what has happened. To be safe, let's jump in a lifeboat, paddle a thousand yards away and watch from a distance. If the

Titanic is OK and she starts to right herself and sail away, we will have to paddle hard to get back onboard, maybe spend some time and money, but at least we know the boat is not going to sink."

Which captain would you rather listen to? I'd pick Captain B.

Dollar cost averaging is one of the biggest spin jobs on the planet. It's a way not to have to admit someone has made a mistake by keeping you in a stock as it goes down, but to turn the mistake into a positive and get you to buy more and even earn another commission.

You must ask your adviser, "If you are so sure the stock is cheap now, why didn't you know when it was more expensive and get me out?" Citigroup may have looked cheap when it hit fifteen dollars a share in October 2008, but if you ponied up more cash and doubled down—as in dollar cost averaging—you probably felt sick to your stomach when it dropped another 93% and hit $0.97 a mere five months later.

Successful traders have a general rule. Never throw good money after bad. Now I'm not implying everyone should be a stock trader, but if you are in a position and that position goes down 8%, move back to cash and re-evaluate. If you lose 8%, you only have to make back 8.7% to get back to even. If you lose 30%, you have to earn back 42.9%. If you lose 50%, you have to earn back 100%. If the old saying is true that the markets always average 10%; losing 8% means you'll wait less than a year to make it back. That sounds better than waiting four to ten years to make back losses.

Remember, you can always go back into a stock position. An analogy I use is the one about the forest and the trees. The idea is to pull back from the trees to see the forest, go to cash and clear your head. Then when you see the forest is burning down, you know to go and invest in fire extinguishers.

"Look how much money I made you last year!"

This one is great. When the markets go up, everyone thumps their chest to proclaim their brilliance. At the beginning of 2007, numerous clients came in declaring their advisors made them 10% in 2006 and were brilliant. My typical response was, "How much did you pay them? And were they so brilliant as to underperform the S&P500, which averaged 15.86%?"

The funny thing, in 2008, generally the opposite was heard.

"It's not my fault; everyone lost money in 2008!"

It is your advisor's fault if you lost money, unless of course you directed your advisor, to their written objections, to buy XYZ and it lost money. We hire mechanics to fix our cars and keep them running. If the car breaks and the mechanic can't or won't fix it, we fire him. How many people stay with their financial advisors as their losses mount and their net worth drops?

In Summary
Warren Buffet has two important rules:
#1 – Don't lose money
#2 – Don't forget #1.

- Consistency is far more important than hitting home runs. Lots of singles and doubles will always win more games than the occasional home run followed by twenty strikeouts.

- Wealth building has always been about having time on your side and allowing the inflationary effects of our government's actions to increase your nest egg.

- Tangible assets can protect you in good times and bad, as long as you follow the simple "L" rules. Keep your debt low and long, keep your cash flow high, and keep a reasonable emergency account in the bank for the rainy days.

"L" Rules said another way:
Low Debt;
Long-term Debt;
Lots of positive cash flow;
Lots of cash in the bank.

Following these simple rules has put more millions in more millionaires' pockets than any other concept. We've all read about the guy who leveraged himself 100%, bet the farm, and won the lotto on an investment. Some people have come out smelling like a rose even though they took humongous risks, but the majority of us aren't so lucky. We will be burned far more often than we are willing to admit.

————

Chapter 5
Leaks in the Bucket

Imagine you're in the desert. Your car has broken down, and you need to fill the radiator with water. Your family is getting hot sitting in the car, but fortunately, you see a gas station just a short walk away. You grab your handy bucket out of the trunk and head out to fill it with water. After finding the water pump, you start to fill your bucket. Soon, you notice the water level in the bucket isn't rising, although the water is flowing into the bucket. You then notice your toes are starting to squish inside your shoes and that there are several small leaks in your bucket and the water is draining out as fast as it is pouring in.

Everyone has a bucket that represents his or her financial net worth. Everything you own, your income, liabilities, taxes, and investments, makes up your financial bucket. As can happen to any bucket, leaks prevent the bucket from serving its purpose. The benefit of a leak-proof financial bucket is to hold and preserve your wealth and hopefully to allow it to expand and grow.

Most people have numerous leaks in their financial bucket. These leaks vary in size, but the result is the same. They prevent you from filling up your financial bucket efficiently. Three financial quarts poured in and one quart leaking out, or in too many instances, people's financial buckets are more like three quarts in and four quarts out. Most people are going backwards.

Common leaks in one's financial bucket are caused by limited investment diversification and taking on too much risk; inflation, hidden investment fees, and taxes; withdrawing too much income from a portfolio, and poor estate planning.

These leaks threaten to drain your financial bucket over time, forcing you to either save more, work harder or for a longer period of time, or risk running out of money. Choices that are never fun and make retirement planning more difficult.

Limited Investment Diversification
This is a brief overview and is discussed in greater detail in Chapter 6.

Most financial programs, magazines, newspapers, blogs, etc. say to be diversified you need many types of stocks, bonds, mutual funds, and some even add annuities to the mix.

Most advisors offer only these asset classes due to their training and limited exposure. Many follow educational paths that are very linear. A leads to B leads to C, etc. Also, the majority of financial advisors were trained by the big wire houses and believe these investments are the only games in town. It is always surprising to look in the yellow pages for financial advisors and brokerage firms and note which of these groups really is all that different from the others. They are basically the same.

My background is in science. My undergrad degree is in Biochemistry, and it taught me to think in terms of how the body protects itself from harm, as well as how to look at problems from a different perspective. I think of it as cause and effect. What are the causes we are dealing with today, and what effects are most likely to result?

May I suggest a homework assignment? Ask your advisor a simple question. "What is going on today, and how is my portfolio designed to withstand any problems on the horizon?" Sit back and critique the answer. If it is unresponsive or sounds similar to the sound bites you've heard on CNBC, maybe it is time to find another advisor who spends more time reading about what's going on in the economy and the world as it relates to finance, and who manages your portfolio accordingly. Advisers are paid for this very purpose, aren't they? They must have a deep knowledge of what is going on in finance today!

Here's an example of how the body protects itself and how we apply this cause and effect concept to finance. If a guy goes outside in only his boxers and falls asleep in a lawn chair on a sunny day, we know what will probably be the outcome. One, his neighbors will probably call the cops, and two, he'll have a painful sunburn. It won't make sitting on the cold concrete in jail very comfortable.

What has happened to him? He has damaged his skin all the way down to the DNA. The four base pairs of DNA are Adenine, Guanine, Cytosine, and Thymine. These are the building blocks of the DNA double helix. The problem with a sunburn, or more accurately UV exposure, is that it causes the Thymine base pairs to bond together forming what is called a T-T dimer. Long story short, parts that are not supposed to stick together are now sticking together.

The amazing thing about the body is that it has the means to repair itself. Little guys go in and fix the T-T dimer, unstick it so to speak, and we're back to the races. If the little guys that go in to fix the problem don't do the job, our bodies have backup systems to make sure the problem is taken care of.

To relate to this story, the major problem is that most financial advisors believe that stocks, bonds, mutual funds, and annuities are the only game in town. In 2008, it didn't matter what you owned; almost everything was drastically impacted in the second worst year in the history of the stock market.

Clients of all ages were coming in with every type of portfolio imaginable: all stocks, all mutual funds, all bonds, all variable annuities, and every mix in between. They all got hammered. A ninety-two-year-old man came in to my office with a portfolio of muni-bond funds. "Well diversified and ultra conservative," his advisor had told him. The gentleman asked for my opinion. I told him, "If you were well diversified, per your advisor, why then did your portfolio drop from $1,100,000 to $764,000? A drop of over 30%." His answer, "I'm not really diversified, am I?"

Bonds are to Wall Street what CDs are to a bank: the conservative choice and the only choice they have.

The problem again is the point of view of the person defining something as conservative. By early 2009, someone invested in thirty-year Treasury bonds would have lost over 20% year to date. How is that a conservative investment?

I was flying back to L.A. a few years back, and sitting next to me was a pilot returning home. She is not piloting this flight, mind you, just catching a ride home as a fellow passenger. Going from Las Vegas to Los Angeles, we flew over the desert on takeoff. The dry winds really create havoc for most planes, causing a lot of turbulence. I made an interesting observation. My knuckles were dead white, hers a nice mellow shade of pink. In fact, she was sipping a cup of tea, not even appearing to think twice about the rough turbulence we were experiencing. I said to her, "No big deal, huh?" Her response, "A walk in the park. If it gets bad, I'll let you know." Though somewhat comforting, I still had the feeling of pending doom.

Her definition of "turbulence" was very different from mine. I feel most financial advisors' definitions of risk are very different from the average investor's. Most advisors promote their version of conservative, which they say are bonds, variable annuities, or index mutual funds, and when the markets lose 40% and the bonds only lose 15%, then that is a conservative investment.

My definition of a conservative investment is not something that ONLY loses 15–20%!

Inflation

As you read the papers and watch TV, you are bombarded with how low inflation is, yet I see the indent at the bottom of the water bottle getting larger each year and the ice cream and shampoo containers getting smaller and smaller. I was curious about the cereal boxes. They looked the same. Same height, same width. Then I noticed the box was getting progressively thinner. I see movie prices going through the roof and gas prices escalating. Even at the time of this writing, after oil had fallen from a high of $147 to current levels in the $40–$50 range, the price of gas is now roughly 50% higher than it was in 2006, a mere three years later.

What would it cost to purchase the same amount of groceries in 2008 that cost one hundred dollars in 2000? $129, according to the CPI-U for food and beverages.

If you don't have an extra twenty-nine dollars in investments, inflation will have eaten up a good portion of your food budget, and you will need to dig into other reserves just to buy the same things.

Food for thought: A hundred dollars invested in the S&P500, not adjusted for inflation—just net of investment performance between January 1, 2000 and January 1, 2009—would today be worth $71.89. Far short of the $129 you would need to buy your groceries. You're really going to lose weight on this amount of money! An inflation diet, so to speak!

In June 2008, bond expert Bill Gross added his voice to those claiming that the CPI (Consumer Price Index, the measure by which the U.S. government reports inflation) understates the actual rate of inflation. While Gross's analysis refers to factors such as hedonic adjustments and equivalent rental rates, the same gibberish that the Bureau of Labor Statistics (BLS) uses in producing its data, his argument sums up to this: The U.S. makes adjustments to its CPI that many other countries don't, and those adjustments don't reflect reality.

Another viewpoint is displayed in the chart below.

Different ways of measuring inflation

During the Reagan and Clinton administrations, the method of calculating rising prices was altered in ways that lowered the official inflation rate. Below is a calculation of how the inflation rate would look today if it were measured by the former methods.

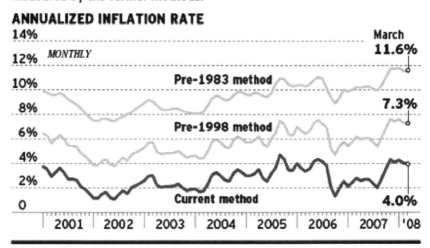

SOURCE: Shadow Government Statistics

2000-June 2008
Source: Reprinted by permission from www.shadowstats.com

The chart above shows an interesting phenomenon. Over different periods, inflation has been calculated in different ways. Using the pre-1983 methodology, inflation for the first half of 2008 would be about 11.6%. Under the Reagan methodology, 1984 to 1998, inflation for 2008 would be 7.6%. Under the Clinton methodology, 1998 to present, inflation was a mere 4.1%.

Even today, using the pre-1983 methodology, inflation would be over 6%.

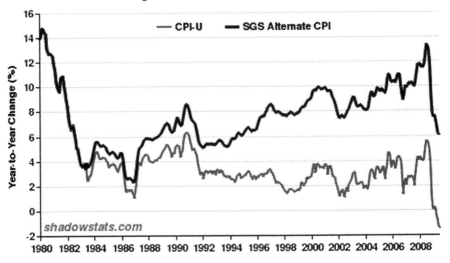

Annual Consumer Inflation - CPI vs SGS Alternate
Through June 2009 (ShadowStats.com, BLS)

1980 to June 2009
Source: Reprinted by permission from www.shadowstats.com

Why was the system to calculate inflation changed? Simple. The United States went from a creditor nation to a debtor nation. Pre-1983, people owed us money. We had a vested interest in showing actual inflation. When countries borrowed from us, we wanted to be paid back in true inflation-adjusted dollars. After Reagan, when we became a net debtor nation, our focus changed to hide inflation. It was in our best interest, since we owed money to other countries. Lastly, 1998 under Clinton, with the unfunded liabilities of the U.S. growing exponentially, the calculation was changed again to hide the real inflation rate. With a lower rate, Social Security checks and Medicare reimbursement rates are lower, and the government can sell Treasury bonds at ridiculously low interest rates to the rest of the world to fund our deficits.

Whether you believe inflation is 4% or 12%, the point is it is very important to understand its effects on your retirement goals and to make sure you are not going backwards in your lifestyle.

The other thing to keep in mind is the unchecked and prolific printing of U.S. Dollars by the Federal Reserve. As consumers stop spending and try to increase their savings, this is counterproductive according to the Federal Reserve, and they are trying to re-inflate prices by running the printing presses at full steam ahead.

Though we might experience price reductions on some capital goods due to a tightening of credit availability, don't be fooled. The U.S. is setting itself up for an inflationary debacle. When people start realizing all these newly printed dollars are eroding their purchasing power, they will stop saving and start converting their money at alarming rates into tangible goods, goods that will preserve their value against a falling dollar. The problem then is the velocity of money shoots through the roof and prices will skyrocket. The velocity of money is defined as the amount of time it takes someone to spend or turn over their money. In normal times, it might take six months to spend a certain amount of money. If the velocity is increasing, they might spend faster, converting dollars into tangible goods, and only take three months to spend the same equivalent amount of money. With the velocity increasing, prices rise quickly due to greater demand for limited supplies.

Case in point, on January 15, 2009, Zimbabwe introduced a $50 billion dollar bill, basically just enough to buy a single loaf of bread. Just three weeks earlier, that same loaf of bread cost a measly $10 billion, and a mere six months before then, it was just $250 Million.

A lady who had all her money in CDs came into my office for a consultation. She asked what the long-term effects of this investment strategy would be.

"Tell me something you like to do," I asked.

"I love the movies. I go twice a week", she replied.

"Great. If you keep all your money in CDs, over time, you will have two choices," I told her. "Your first choice is to reduce your trips to the movies."

"Never," she replied. "I love the movies; I will be going at least twice a week forever."

"Then," I warned her, "choice number two is to go broke."

Over time, her money would fall far short of her actual expenditures. Since she takes out all of her interest from the CDs each year, her principal is not growing, and thus her CDs do not provide increasingly higher interest payments. Look at the price of movies over time. When I was a kid, they were three dollars. I'm sure some of you can recall the time when they were a quarter or even less. Recently, my wife and I went to the theatre, and between the movie price of $14.50 per ticket and one box of popcorn and parking, we were out over forty dollars. We're not in Kansas anymore, Toto.

Investment Fees

A man comes into my office, curious about the fees he is paying in his portfolio. He even called his advisor that morning, and his advisor told him he was in no load mutual funds and annuities and his cost was the 1% annual asset fee.

His portfolio was about $250,000, so his annual fee was $2,500. His portfolio consisted of one hundred thousand dollars sitting in a money market account, one hundred thousand dollars in various no load mutual funds, and fifty thousand dollars in a variable annuity.

Starting with his money market account, I asked him if he could guess the fees he was paying. "Fees, in a money market account? There are no fees!" he told me.

Going online and finding the prospectus for his particular money market account, on the sixth page, the fees of the money market fund were clearly spelled out:

0.5% management fees, 0.25% 12-b-1 fees (marketing expenses, someone has to pay for all those beautiful brochures), and .30% misc. All added together, the fees came to 1.05%. Below this number was a rebate of 0.05% bringing the total to 1%. I guess they did the rebate because they didn't want to seem like they were gouging the client on his savings!

On his hundred thousand dollars in the money market, he was paying one thousand dollars in fees annually, or eighty-three dollars per month.

Surprised, he pulled out the statements for his mutual funds. Using various resources on the web such as Personalfund.com, we broke down each of his funds.

Not only do they have management fees, but also Transaction Costs (these are the buying and selling commissions within the fund itself), 12-b-1 fees, and taxes for holding the fund. Taxes arising from the dividends received or reinvested if held within an after tax account. There are other invisible fees, such as soft dollar arrangements, etc., which are usually buried in the transaction costs. Unfortunately, they don't report the transaction costs anywhere because in theory they don't know what they will be for the upcoming year. How convenient.

The typical fee for this man's mutual funds was 3%. Again, these were no-load mutual funds. All the "no-load" refers to is the upfront commission. It has nothing to do with the ongoing fees, which all funds charge. It is common for an advisor to sell Class-B shares that don't have an upfront fee but include higher ongoing fees. If you ever sell the fund before the surrender period runs out, the remainder of the commission due will be deducted from the proceeds.

For example:
Class A Fund has a 4% upfront commission and a 2% ongoing fee.
Class B Fund has a 0% upfront commission (typical No-Load) but has an ongoing fee of 3.25%.

Note that the advisor is making an extra 1.25% each year for the Class B Fund, and over the course of four years, will have been paid the same as if you had paid the upfront commission. At this point, ethical advisors will convert the B-Shares into A-Shares so that the client isn't paying the higher ongoing fee. The problem is that very few advisors actually convert the shares. Why do it and get paid less, right?

As a rule of rule of thumb, we don't recommend traditional buy and hold mutual funds. If you are going to buy something to hold for a long time, buy Class A shares. Yes, you will pay more upfront, but your ongoing fees will be less.

Finally, the gentleman had a variable annuity for fifty thousand dollars. Right off the bat, he said his variable was earning 7% per year guaranteed.

Before I addressed his statement, I showed him that the Variable Annuity had similar mutual fund costs within the sub-accounts, but there was also an extra layer of fees for the insurance company who issued the annuity.

The fees included Mortality & Expense (M&E) fees of 1.25%. This fee is basically the cost of the death benefit, which in essence will reimburse you for the principal invested if you die still holding the annuity. Said another way, if the variable annuity loses money, you will pay for life insurance to pay back the principal lost if you die still holding the annuity. Great insurance, wouldn't you agree? You pay extra premiums to protect the Insurance Company from losing your money. Hmm, sounds fishy.

Other fees include the bells and whistles, for which these contracts are famous. An example was his statement about his annuity being guaranteed to grow at 7%. Now, I'm sure he is saying exactly what his advisor told him when selling him the annuity. The problem is that the advisor told only part of the story.

His contract was guaranteed to grow by 7% over a ten-year period. But unlike what this man thought, which was that he could pull all the money out with the guaranteed growth at the end of the tenth year, that does not apply if the contract isn't annuitized. Basically, this 7% guaranteed number is only accessible if the man receives payments from the contract over his lifetime or for a minimum of twenty years. How is it possible the insurance group could guarantee a growth of 7%? They knew the only way the man would get it was to leave the money with them for the ten years plus an additional twenty years, for a total of thirty years. This was not what the man understood.

If he pulled out his money at the end of the tenth year, he would receive only what the contract was worth net of investment performance, fees, and withdrawals.

The total fees for this variable annuity averaged 4% or two thousand dollars.

Fee Tally:

1% Advisor Wrap Fee	= $2,500
1% Money Market Fee	= $1,000
3% Mutual Funds	= $3,000
4% Variable Annuity	= $2,000
Total Fees	$7,500 or $625 per month.

Considering this man was living off his dividends, he was shocked to learn that he was paying $625 out of his pocket each month into Wall Street's pocket.

The quickest way to get a reading on the moral character of your advisor is to ask to have the fees broken down in your portfolio and compare them to what you come up with for fees. If they are significantly different, fire your advisor.

Why are fees such a big deal? Everyone deserves to make a living. We hire financial advisers for their expertise and knowledge. They are paid to do a job and deserve to be paid, as does your mechanic or doctor.

The problem is that fees can be a huge leak in the bucket if they are excessively high.

On a typical mutual fund held for ten years, where fees average between 2–3% with all the hidden stuff added back in, it means you will pay approximately 20–30% out of your pocket to Wall Street just to cover fees. As of early 2009, the stock market had essentially gone sideways for twelve years, yet most people's portfolios were nowhere close to the level they were in 1997 due to the fees paid. If you factor in the effects of inflation, the results where even more grim.

Take a look at your retirement funds. Have you ever wondered why you have so few choices in your 401K, 403B, 457, etc., etc.? When the plan was first presented to your employer, often the choices in the plan were picked to provide the best return possible for the provider of the mutual funds. Wait, isn't that supposed to be the best possible return for the employee? Hardly. Most funds underperform the S&P500 in time spans of five years or longer. If they truly were looking out for you, they would just have you invest in general index funds with low turnover and low expense ratios.

Who do you think worked so hard to get your money into the various retirement funds? Wall Street! Most people in the 1950s had pensions, and Wall Street couldn't get their greedy little hands on the money, so they fought the good fight and finally won additional retirement choices for you to put in your pre-tax dollars from work. Now, they could charge their fees and all the while fill our heads with propaganda that the stock market was the only game in town. No wonder they have been fighting to privatize social security for fifty years. They would love to get their hands and fees on the giant trust account.

On an aside, there is an eternal debate over fee-only advisors and commission-based advisors. Fee-only advisors being advisors who charge a fixed amount for designing a financial plan, say five thousand dollars, and market themselves as an unbiased resource. We tend to think of fee-only advisors as a bit hypocritical. If you walk in and pay five thousand dollars for a comprehensive plan by a fee-only advisor, you obviously trust this person to guide you accurately.

Once you have this magical plan in your hands, the dilemma then becomes how do you implement the plan? Who can put all the pieces together and turn the plan into the pot of gold at the end of the rainbow? Naturally, you want to trust the person who designed the plan and will probably end up back at his or her door to implement it, thus the hypocrisy of fee-only advisors. They take off their fee-only hat and put on their commission hat to put the financial investments in place and earn a second round of compensation.

The best advisors are paid a combination of these types of compensation models and are upfront about it. It is the only way to effectively help people invest their money. By not forcing one payment model over the other, an advisor can pick the ideas that make the most sense for the client, instead of for the advisor's business model.

Income, Income, Income
How often have you heard that a reasonable withdrawal rate from a portfolio is around 4%? Study after study shows that pulling out more than this amount in a portfolio of stocks and bonds will likely erode the principal in the long run and risk your retirement nest egg.

We propose that stock portfolios, and now with rising interest rates for the foreseeable future, bond portfolios, ARE NOT designed for generating income and SHOULD ONLY be used for growth purposes and liquidity needs.

Wall Street will always tell you that the markets average 10%. This is not true. The S&P500 from January 1871 to January 2009 has averaged 8.6%, with full dividend reinvestment. If you were taking out dividends for income, then the S&P500 returned a measly 3.89%. Far short of the magic 10% number.

What most advisors don't know or frankly ignore is that there have been periods when the S&P500 averaged 0%. During the previous and long bear markets, 1881–1921, 1929–1954, and 1965–1982, these were periods in history when you made nothing in the stock market.

The cover of *Business Week*, August 1979, said it best: "The Death of Equities." Why? Because the markets had gone up and down for the previous fourteen years like a roller coaster and kept returning to where they began.

The inherent problem with pulling income from equity portfolios is the compounded effect in bad years.

Assume the markets go back and forth for several years in a row: 10% up and 10% down. Back and forth, back and forth.

Typical side ways pattern in bear market.

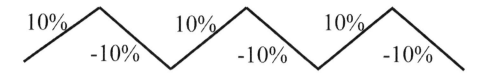

Each year, you pull out the same amount of income from your account. How about the universal 4% that Wall Street recommends?

On top of the 4% you are taking for income, assume your fees are 2% a year.

The long-term effect is that the growth of your account is stunted in the good years and the losses are compounded in the bad years.

In the good years, you make 10% but then take out 4% for income and 2% for fees, leaving only 4% overall growth in the account.

In the bad years, you lose 10%, and with the 4% withdrawal for income and 2% fees, your overall portfolio has dropped 16%. This path is unsustainable, and before long, you will run out of money.

Typical side ways pattern in bear market.

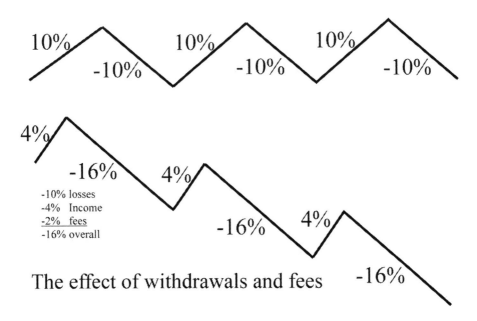

10%   10%   10%
-10%   -10%   -10%

4%
-16%   4%
-10% losses
-4% Income
-2% fees
-16% overall
-16%   4%
-16%

The effect of withdrawals and fees

There is another dilemma people face when using equity portfolios for income needs. It is their flight or fight emotional response.

When the market is going down, the flight or fight response kicks in, and people usually feel a lot of stress when pulling money out of their accounts. They don't want to compound the losses and thus will sacrifice their standard of living so as not to pull out too much from their accounts. Then in good years, they often will take out too much because they feel they are making up for a bad year, and thus, they diminish the long-term growth possibility of their nest egg.

The result is the same: a lot of unnecessary stress because their money has been positioned in the wrong type of investments to meet their goals. The best investments for income purposes are the ones designed to provide high income streams without causing wide swings in the principal balance.

Many of the investments we'll discuss in Chapters 6 and 7 are investments that are designed to generate high cash flow, and since the principal is not tied to the stock market, you don't see wild fluctuations in price. When investments are not subject to wild fluctuations, people tend not to panic, and they allow their money to work over time. One of the biggest reasons most investments don't work out is due to the fear/greed cycle and irrationality of buy/sell decisions. Buy high, sell low.

Taxes

A giant leak in the bucket is taxes. Everything from income to estate taxes is a drain on your wealth bucket each year, and even after you kick the bucket. Uncle Sam is always looking for his take. There is nothing wrong with that, but to quote Author Godfrey, "I'm proud of paying taxes; the only thing: I could be just as proud for half the money."

Pay the tax you are legally obligated to pay, just don't leave a tip!

Most people depend so heavily on their CPA for tax advice that they forget this person is so bogged down with all the duties of just figuring out their tax bill that he or she doesn't usually spend a lot of time helping clients truly reduce their tax bills. That is a job for the financial advisor. Yet, how many people can think of a sit-down with their advisor where they discussed tax strategies?

Most advisors will never bring it up because they aren't paid a commission for discussing taxes, so why bother?

Our reason for helping clients think outside the box is simple. Take care of the client, and they will take care of you. If I can show a client how to save ten thousand dollars in taxes by using a simple C-Corp for their business and deducting some expenses they were paying with after-tax dollars, they now have an extra ten thousand dollars in their pocket for their enjoyment, not Uncle Sam's. What might the client use the newfound ten thousand dollars for? If they don't plan on spending it, maybe they hand it back to us for investment purposes. What goes around comes around.

On the topic of CPAs, EAs, and so forth, these people are a vital part of your financial team, but please understand their general background. They are tax pros. Many times, clients will say, "I have to consult with my CPA on whether this investment makes any sense." I encourage it but also jokingly say, "After you consult with your tax person, you should consult with your mechanic and maybe even your doctor."

The reason I say this is that your mechanic and doctor probably know as much about these investments as your CPA does, so their opinions are probably just as valid. Your CPA may not understand these investments, and in turn give terrible advice because he has no idea what we're talking about. He may even automatically say that the investment is bad. If you think about their Errors and Omission insurance, it only covers tax issues, not investment advice. If a CPA is being cautious, it is in their best interest to recommend against these ideas because if something does happen in the future, they can come back and say they didn't recommend the investment and it is not their fault. The best CPAs will generally be upfront about this issue. They will say something like, "The investment is outside my area of expertise; you should consult with other financial advisors to get an informed second opinion."

If you feel you need a second opinion on an investment portfolio or idea and are not sure who to ask for another opinion, feel free to call us at Vanclef Financial Group, 800-737-8552, or go to our website at www.VFGroup. net. We'll be happy to give you our two cents worth.

Taxes and investments go hand in hand. Many of the best investments have huge tax savings tied to them. For example, you have a small rental house, and in a given year, you receive ten thousand dollars in rental income. That same year on your tax return, you deduct the depreciation of the house, for instance ten thousand dollars, against the rental income. In this situation, you have enjoyed ten thousand dollars of rental income in your pocket and do not have to pay a dime in income taxes.

Compare that to the person who has ten thousand dollars in CD interest income. If they were in the 30% tax bracket, they would only have seven thousand dollars to enjoy after the three thousand dollars in taxes due.

Now, the person who was able to use depreciation to offset the rental income will have a lower cost basis for their rental property, but if they eventually sell the investment home and use a 1031 tax deferred exchange to get into another property, no tax will be due. If that person eventually passes away, they will receive a step-up in the cost basis of the investment home, and the capital gains and recapture taxes that were due disappear. This is one way the rich get richer. They understand the wealth code on taxes and how to best preserve their nest eggs and pass them from generation to generation without the government stealing half.

Poor Estate Planning
How is it possible for someone like Henry J. Kaiser, Jr., to die with an estate of $55,910,373 and only lose $1,030,415 in estate costs, when someone like Elvis Presley, who died with only $10,165,434 loses $7,374,635 or

73% to estate costs and taxes? The difference is estate planning, another huge leak in the bucket.

Most people do not realize the implications of death on an estate. Usually, something as simple as a living trust in the appropriate states or wills in those states where those are more appropriate would save countless hours of aggravation and money drained from the estate in court fees, attorneys fees, and so forth.

One reason people give for not having the proper estate plans put in place is the cost. This is unfortunate and shortsighted.

One client with an estate over $15 million called me after sitting with a highly qualified estate tax attorney I recommended. He told me he was outraged by the price the attorney would charge to implement a solid estate plan. In this case, the total cost was about eight thousand dollars. I reminded the client that he would be saving about $3 million in estate taxes by using the plan. Still, the client was so focused on the "outrageous" eight thousand dollars that he never implemented the plan.

Penny wise and pound foolish, as the saying goes. By focusing only on the cost, the client lost sight on the goal. Said another way, would you invest eight thousand dollars in a mutual fund if it was assured of returning $3 million in profits? Of course, this is a no brainer. Why then would it be unthinkable to spend eight thousand dollars on attorneys' fees up front to get a big binder of paperwork that in the long run would save $3 million in estate taxes?

A good exercise is to ask yourself two or three questions, depending on your situation.

If you are single:
1. What happens financially if you are incapacitated tomorrow and cannot work?
2. What happens to your loved ones financially if you die tomorrow?

If you are married:
1. What happens financially if you or your spouse becomes incapacitated tomorrow and cannot work?
2. What happens to your spouse financially and estate-tax wise if you die tomorrow?

3. What happens to your children or beneficiaries once the second of the spouses passes away, in terms of taxes and financial well-being?

Most people have never asked themselves these questions. It can be difficult to talk about such things as becoming incapacitated or dying. It's easier to push that topic to another day.

There is a saying that the only thing in life that is guaranteed is that tomorrow is not guaranteed!

People usually say death AND taxes are inevitable, but I'm not so sure about the taxes, with proper estate and income tax planning.

Here's a sad reality. In California, if you have an estate that exceeds the federal estate tax exemption, $3.5 million in 2009, every dollar in a retirement account will shrink by roughly 91% when the person dies.

If, and most do, a beneficiary pulls all the money out to cash from an inherited retirement account such as an IRA, 401K, etc., the income tax will be paid as well as the Federal Estate Tax, and the beneficiary will be left with a piddly 9%.

If one hundred dollars in a 401K becomes nine dollars after all taxes are paid, how is that for a leak in the bucket? This is another example of poor estate planning. A better solution would be to plan for the problems the retirement account would pose after a death of the account owner, and start unwinding the account completely to after-tax accounts and possibly obtain insurance, so the proceeds would be estate and income tax-free.

Liquidity

Every day, you hear the importance of liquidity with your money. A more complete description of this leak will be covered in Chapter 6, but for now, a simple discussion will suffice.

While giving presentations at night to clients and potential clients, I used to ask for a show of hands. Who has had a fifty-thousand-dollar emergency that required you to pull out money the very next day? This emergency does not include medical bills, which can be paid over time or a new car purchase on a whim, but something tragic, like your mean uncle has been kidnapped and you need fifty thousand dollars in cash the next day to save him.

People always say they have tons of money in the bank for that "what if" emergency. The problem is that those "what if" emergencies rarely, if ever, happen, and you are stuck with money sitting in the bank earning nothing. You are incurring opportunity costs. That money could be working harder for you, but since you keep a large chunk for that rare emergency, you rationalize to yourself it is ok to earn 1% because it is for peace of mind.

I have asked this question of over ten thousand people who attended my workshops over the years, and only six people ever raised their hands. Some people were at the thirty-thousand-dollar level, and more at the twenty- or ten-thousand-dollar level, but rarely at the fifty-thousand-dollar amount. They just haven't experienced such emergencies.

Wall Street will always say that an investment that is liquid is usually considered a better investment than one that is not. I disagree. Liquidity to me means the investment is far more prone to emotional decisions, i.e. decisions made under duress or panic. For instance, when the markets are getting killed, people are always heard saying they sold at the bottom, right before the market turned up. As of this writing, the Dow Jones Industrial Average is at 6629 on March 7, 2009. In the papers, everyone is screaming about the average going to 3000 or 2500, the previous support levels dating back to 1984. The sad part is, we are probably at the bottom of the downturn of the market. When people become so afraid and everyone is selling, that is usually the time to buy.

Illiquid investments provide a buffer from the irrational decisions we humans are prone to make. Since one can't sell even when all seems lost, the investments will usually have time to regain any lost value and become profitable.

A good example would be the drop in value owners experienced on their personal residences bought pre-1990, the last residential real estate market top. Most homes decreased in value from 1990–1994, but because it wasn't easy to sell a home due to the general illiquidity, owners ended up riding it out, and over time, the house became worth a lot more. An advantage of owning tangible investments, as long as you are not forced to sell in the bad times, is their ability to appreciate in value over time due to inflation.

The illiquidity of the home provided a buffer, making it difficult to sell at the bottom, say in 1994, preventing the owner from making a bad investment choice. Stocks don't have the luxury of being illiquid. They can be sold on a whim, which often leads to those who buy the tops with emotional greed and those sell the bottoms with emotional panic.

Let us re-address this enormous leak in the bucket, liquidity, in Chapter 6, after a more complete discussion of the different investment classes available to you and the general characteristics of each one.

Summary: Leaks in the Bucket

We all have financial buckets that represent our net worth. Unfortunately, we also have numerous leaks in our buckets that drain off money each year and reduce the size of our nest eggs. Leaks include everything from taxes, estate planning, limited investment choices, and fees. Fortunately, once the leaks are identified, you can begin plugging them. As more and more of the leaks get plugged, you will find that your bucket will fill up more quickly with even the slightest gains. Recognizing the problem is the hardest part, but that is the purpose for the solutions we present in the upcoming chapters.

———

Chapter 6
True Asset Class Diversification

In the beginning, we introduced the chart of all the investment classes into which you can invest your hard earned money. We talked about why the Olympic basketball team could still win the gold medal even though one of its stars, Kobe, was not on the court.

Below is a simple description of the general asset classes. These descriptions will be covered in greater detail in Chapter 7.

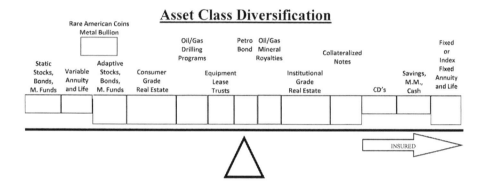

Static Stocks, Bonds, Mutual Funds
This category includes any stock, bond, mutual fund, or derivative that is held over one year. I call this the-hope-and-pray leg on the financial table. The vast majority of investors only know this asset class. This class tends to do well in bull markets. The problem since 2000, however, is that we have been in a bear market. In fact, as of this writing in early 2009, the markets are at the same place they were twelve years prior.

Variable Annuities
These are essentially the same as static accounts, except they offer more bells and whistles and generally include more fees associated with them.

Adaptive Managed Stocks and Bonds
This category includes investment managers who take an active role in changing the portfolio throughout the year to adapt to what is going on in the economy and world. The managers we tend to recommend essentially rebuild the portfolios from scratch every quarter and do not have restrictions in terms of which type of equity classes they can use to build the overall

portfolio. For instance, they can use bonds, stocks, or commodities. They have the ability to mix and match any of the three equity classes as they see fit. The main criteria for these advisors we hire is that they cannot use leverage. They work with all cash, which eliminates hedge funds.

Side note: How many times did your investment advisor change your portfolio in the year 2008? How many times did he or she even call you in 2008?

Consumer Grade Real Estate
In general, real estate valued at $10 million or less, including residential homes and apartment buildings as well as small commercial properties, is considered Consumer Grade Real Estate. Their prices tend to fluctuate far more than prices for large commercial properties because the buyers are generally less sophisticated than a group purchasing say a $100 million property. More emotion is involved, which causes larger increases in good years but more significant drops in bad years.

Rare American Coins
Metal Bullion falls into this category, but for our discussions, we prefer Rare Coins, which have a higher multiple against inflation. That is, for instance, if gold went up 50%, rare coins in general might have a 100% appreciation.

Oil/Gas Investments
These include everything from exploration and developmental to royalty programs.

Exploration Programs – New wells in uncharted areas. In general, these were the majority of the programs in the '80s, which everyone remembers lost the most money. They tend to have a very low success rate.

Developmental Programs – New or reconditioned wells in existing fields around existing producing wells. Think of an oil/gas field with lots of wells already producing. These programs are putting more straws in the dirt. Common drilling success rates can be in the upper 90% range.

Royalty Programs – Buying land with mineral rights and letting the developmental or exploratory drillers do all the hard work. For their hard work, they generally get 75% of the production. Royalty owners sit back and collect 25% of the production coming from their lands. This is considered the most conservative form of direct ownership energy investing.

Equipment Leases

Companies that specialize in purchasing and leasing equipment to other companies and then sell that equipment after the lease period.

Energy Bonds

Essentially, these include notes collateralized with energy investments and distributions. The common sense idea behind these bonds is they are interest rate positive. That is, when interest rates go up, in general, commodities go up, and thus energy bonds become more secure. Traditional debt instruments are interest rate negative. That is, when interest rates go up, the bond's principal goes down.

Institutional Grade Real Estate

This is generally real estate valued at $10 million or more, either single or portfolio properties, Tenant-in-Common, or non-traded REITs. The key to the REITs in this category is that they are NOT on the stock market. The REITs that trade on the stock market are classified as Static Mutual funds. Though they are real estate, since they trade on the markets, they tend to follow the markets in general and lose much of their non-correlation status. Also, the way stock market REITs raise cash is very different from the way non-traded REITs raise cash.

Collateralized Notes

These, in a nut shell, are debt instruments collateralized by real estate. They can be first, second, or greater position deeds. As a rule, our firm only represents first position notes.

Certificates of Deposit

Bank instruments that are FDIC insured. This category includes a new investment vehicle called structured CDs. These CDs are tied to a stock market index with guarantees of principal.

Cash

Bank instruments that are FDIC insured.

Fixed Annuity

Either fixed or index fixed, these are similar in design to variable annuities from an insurance standpoint. They include the same types of annuitization features, income riders, and bonuses, yet not in the market. Recently, the

SEC ruled that index fixed annuities, since they correspond to various market indexes, are now considered securities and must be sold by licensed individuals. We feel this is an important change in the index annuity arena because many insurance-only agents have represented themselves as full service advisors, discussing the stock market in general yet not having any of the required licenses.

The last category that has not been discussed is life insurance as an investment. Life insurance has many purposes, and many different advisors use it depending on their viewpoint. Some only sell life insurance so that two years down the road they can sell the policy in the settlement market for a cash payout. Others use it for estate planning purposes, and others use it as a long-term retirement vehicle. These are a few of the uses for life insurance and have their advantages as well as pitfalls. In Chapter 9, we will discuss our viewpoint of the various ideas we see coming across our desk. Insurance is a very important part of financial planning for some people, but it doesn't make sense for others. It depends on the client and their needs.

This has been just a brief overview of the different asset classes. In Chapter 7, we will provide more detailed explanations of the different asset classes.

The goal of the next sections is to provide a different viewpoint on money, a point of view that we think is simple to grasp yet powerful to know. Most people will tell you that finance is too complicated. I remember a fellow advisor who once told a client that if they could make a children's book out of Einstein's theory of relativity, then teaching people about finance should be a walk in the park.

Let's start with the view at twenty thousand feet and begin to look at money in terms of general groupings.

The investments on the left side of the teeter-totter below are generally Emotional Investments. They trade, and their prices fluctuate based on fear and greed. The general public has the ultimate control. When they get greedy, the prices tend to jump quickly. Of course, when fear sets in, prices tend to drop far faster. Why? Fear is a more powerful emotion than greed.

The investments on the right side of the teeter-totter tend to be Unemotional Investments. A CD is a good example. You buy a CD, assume 4% for one year, and over the duration of one year you will earn 4%. There isn't a lot to worry about with a CD, unless of course the bank you have your money in goes belly up. Even though you are probably within the FDIC's limits, no matter what people say, it is still unnerving to be in a bank that becomes insolvent.

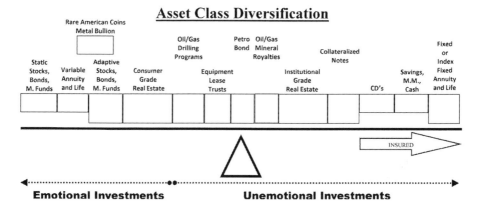

Coming down to the ten-thousand-foot level, investments can generally be thought of in three categories:

High Return (HR)	Goal of 10% or more per year;
Liquid (L)	Access to all your money essentially the next day;
Capital Preservation (CP)	The reasonable assumption your money is protected and the balance won't fluctuate much if at all.

There is a fourth description that applies to fixed annuities or index fixed annuities, and that is:

Mid-Return (MR) – Goal of 3–6% per year.

Fixed annuities are meant for someone who is looking for very specific goals. We don't feel they will keep up with inflation in the long run and thus are not part of the three main groupings. Annuities do serve a purpose, however, and will be discussed in Chapter 9.

With Preservation, as always, assumptions must be made. The key word is REASONABLE assumptions. For instance, let's say a particular oil royalty program effectively pays 5% at thirty dollars per barrel oil. At forty dollars, the dividends will effectively be around 8%. At sixty-dollar oil, the dividends can be around 14%. No two royalty programs are the same, and there is never a guarantee of dividends or return of principal. With that being said, after some detailed due diligence on the group that is bringing out the royalty program, let's say you feel the above dividends will generally match those oil prices. The overall assumption that needs to follow is your own. If you personally think oil is going down to five dollars, then you would never want to get into this particular investment. On the flip side, if you believe oil is going to eighty dollars and will at least stay above thirty dollars for the foreseeable future, then you believe your dividends should be 5% and more. You would be going into the investment with eyes open and reasonable assumptions being made.

The catch to all investments in general is that you can have ONLY two of the three descriptors per investment.

There is no such thing as an investment that meets all three goals: High Return, Liquid, and offers Capital Preservation. If someone tells you about an investment with all three general descriptions, I have a great bridge in Brooklyn to sell you.

Goal: **High Return and Liquid**
Trade off: **Capital Preservation**

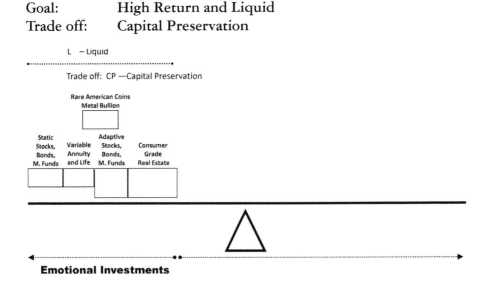

As a group, investments that fall into the emotional category tend to be described as High Return and Liquid.

Stocks and bonds can be thought of as high return and liquid, as can consumer grade real estate and rare coins. But the trade off to these investments is you give up the preservation of your capital and take on increased volatility and risk of principal. Between October 2008 and February 2009, it's interesting to observe that there were more plus/negative 5% moves in the stock market during those four months than in the previous fifty years combined. It gives new meaning to volatility and high risk.

You might think to yourself, "My bonds are conservative and they preserve my capital." Do they? In January 2009, Treasury bonds sustained their biggest losses in U.S. history, around 12%. That's a loss of 12% in a single month. Does that sound like an investment that preserves one's capital? Bonds perform well in an environment of falling interest rates, such as we had between 1982 and 2002, but since then, we've basically been in a rising interest rate environment. If history is any guide, these secular or long-term interest rate trends move in roughly twenty-year cycles. If the rising rate cycle started in 2002, we are going to see interest rates move in the wrong direction for bonds for many years to come.

Goal: **High Return and Capital Preservation**
Trade off: **Liquidity**

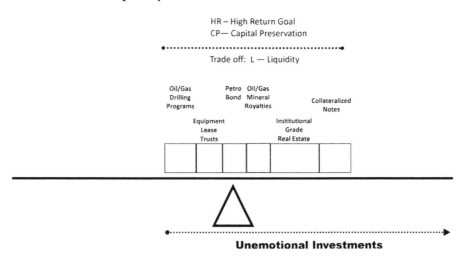

The investments in the middle of the teeter-totter are as follows: Oil/Gas, Institutional Grade Real Estate, Equipment Leases, and Collateralized Notes. These generally fall into the high return and capital preservation category, but the catch to these investments is that you give up liquidity.

The key to these investments is Time and Collateral. There is something backing the money that in general provides an inflation hedge. Look at the wealth of the very rich. The majority of it was built from tangible assets: real estate, oil/gas, timber, or they built a business.

When Enron went out of business, the stockholders lost everything. The bond holders lost everything. Who didn't lose? The real estate group that owned the Enron headquarters building. They lost a tenant and some rent for a while. But, as soon as they got new tenants, they were back in business.

If Fed Ex were to go out of business, the stock and bond holders would get nothing. The Equipment Leasing group that owns the plane Fed Ex is using would simply take back the plane, paint it brown, call it UPS, and re-lease it. Then they would sue Fed Ex for the difference in lost lease payments.

The bottom line is that there is more than a promise and a stock certificate backing the investment.

Many will argue that stocks over time will provide the same inflation hedge. I disagree. As reported in a 2009 Study from DALBAR, Inc., a Boston based research firm:

"From January 1, 1989 to December 31, 2008, the average equity investor earned 1.87% annually: compared to inflation of 2.89% and the 8.35% that the S&P 500 index earned annually for that 20 year time period."

"The average fixed income investor earned 0.77% annually; compared to the Barclays Aggregate Bond Index at 7.43%."

"In fact, in all three categories of average investors, they saw negative returns in all holding periods (1, 3, 5, and 10) except the 20-year time frame. And even those long-term results were paltry—less than the official inflation rate."

DALBAR studied the cash inflows and outflows of the market, over these time periods, which demonstrate the emotional buying and selling of the typical investor. Buying at the top (Greed) and selling the bottom (Fear) dramatically affected the long-term performance results of their portfolios.

The table below shows the various holding periods and the results for the average investor.

	20 Year	10 Year	5 Year	3 Year	1 Year
Equity	1.87%	-1.57%	-2.84%	-10.38%	-41.63%
Fixed Income	0.77%	-0.66%	-1.84%	-3.56%	-11.71%
Asset Allocation*	1.67%	-1.26%	-2.89%	-7.72%	-30.04%

Asset Allocation being 60% stocks and 40% bonds

Now that you've seen the results, perhaps you're wondering why investors have done so poorly in achieving returns in line with two of the most popular benchmarks. Well, we believe the answer stems from one main issue: emotion.

Buying high and selling low. Wall Street preaches the opposite, but in practice, few people achieve great results in the markets. Few people have the patience to ride out the rough times.

When the going gets tough, many people panic. They sell at the wrong times, miss rebounds, and buy at the emotional tops before the next correction, further compounding poor performance.

Yet, most people swear up, down, and sideways that they are making money hand over fist. Over the years, as thousands of people have met across my desk and discussed their investments, they tend to exaggerate dramatically the performance of their portfolio. They probably do this to justify the years they have been in the markets.

A gentleman came in and said, "Morgan Stanley did a great job. I started with three hundred thousand dollars twelve years ago. I've pulled out over two hundred thousand dollars, and I still have $280,000 today. My advisor says I've averaged over 10%." It is easy to say something, and most investors lack the tools to double-check a statement made to them about their performance results.

My favorite side companion is my HP10bII calculator. It's a very simple financial calculator to use, and I strongly suggest anyone who wants to have a clearer picture of their finances pick one up and learn simple calculations like future value, interest earned, and so forth.

Handing it to the man, I had him punch in the appropriate numbers.

Starting principal: $300,000
Ending principal: $280,000
Time: 12 years
Payments received: $200,000 at $16,667 per year
Solve for the Interest earned: 5.14%

I asked him whether he likes watching his accounts go up and down, and he responded that he hated it. The stress drove him nuts. The realization that he had made basically what a CD would have paid over the same period of time eroded his belief in the stock market.

A doctor came in raving about the great performance of his mutual funds within his 401K. "I started with one hundred thousand dollars, and today I have two hundred thousand dollars in my accounts a mere five years later. Can you match that?" he asked. I then pointed out that his statements showed he had contributed another one hundred thousand dollars over that five-year period, in addition to the hundred thousand dollars he started with. He looked sternly at me and said, "I'm too busy working to make any money!"

Goal: **Capital Preservation and Liquidity**
Trade off: **High Return**

CP— Capital Preservation
L — Liquidity

Trade off: HR — High Return

Savings,
M.M.,
CD's   Cash

INSURED

Unemotional Investments

Investments in this category are generally the banking and brokerage products: CDs, savings, cash, and money market accounts. These investments are generally for emergencies and short-term financial goals. We've described these investments to clients as short-term parking spots.

If you park a car on a street and forget about it for a week, what happens? You get a ticket, or worse, your car gets towed.

The penalty you incur for keeping your money in these investment products is that you are losing to inflation. Your purchasing power on the dollars in these investments is going down, thus the joke, "Certificates of Depreciation." The only decade when CDs have outpaced inflation and taxes was the 1980s, and only by a smidgen.

In 1980, inflation spiked to over 13.5% while a six-month CD paid on average 12.94%. The owners of these CDs actually lost 0.56% in purchasing power that year because of inflation. To put this in actual dollars, if you had put ten thousand dollars into a CD, your statement at the end of the year would have shown a balance of $11,294. It looks pretty good. The problem is that $11,294 would only buy $9,951 worth of goods in terms of the previous year's dollars. Worse yet, if you were in the 20% tax bracket and 4% state tax bracket, now you would be down to $9,677. The inflation diet is having a powerful, negative impact on your savings.

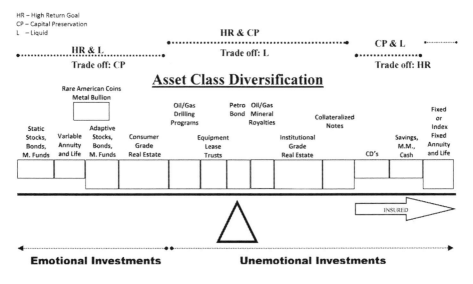

Looking at the teeter-totter, we want to give you a way to look at your money from a new perspective and show you how to build a solid financial table.

We feel the best portfolios are mixtures of these investment categories, having money in the HR-L bucket, as well as the HR-CP bucket and CP-L bucket. You never want one or the other. Liquidity, though often overstated in terms of necessity, is important for part of your money. High return is vital to keep up with the hidden tax of inflation, and preservation of your capital is the foundation for the other two.

In general, we believe moving people away from static stocks, bonds, and mutual funds, as well as from variable annuities down the teeter-totter is important for achieving the goals of most investors. Some of the money in the CP-L category can be moved a little bit up the teeter-totter because you can be too safe with your money and lose to inflation.

Sometimes, people will move from this category down the teeter-totter into the fixed annuity asset class. Although moving from other categories into the fixed annuity asset class will not keep up with inflation in the long run, it is sometimes what is needed. There are times when it is appropriate to provide a high degree of protection and the tax deferred attributes of a fixed annuity, or the pension-like payouts that are possible under an annuity.

A rule of thumb we use is one-third in the High Return-Liquidity bucket (the emotional investments, not counting your personal residence) and two-thirds in the other categories.

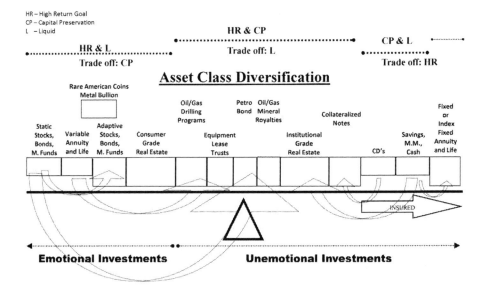

Each person is different, and their situation ultimately determines the appropriate buckets into which their money is placed. Sit down with your advisor and find placements appropriate for you.

A guy comes in for a consultation. I notice he has 100% of his money (over a million) in his checking account. After listening to him and his lifestyle choices, I encouraged him to put his money into a higher insured deposit account, up to $50 million, and wished him well. Most people would think this was lousy advice. He is losing to inflation; his money is not growing at all. Yes, your arguments are all correct.

The man was a bit eccentric. The greatest pleasure he had in his life was going to an ATM, withdrawing twenty dollars, then leaving the ATM slip on the counter and watching from a distance as the next passerby who used the ATM would notice the slip and the large amount and then possibly look around to see who was Mr. or Ms. Big Bucks. He would do this five to ten times per day for the pure enjoyment of seeing the reaction on people's faces as they noticed the big dollar amount.

To each his own. . .

Liquidity Leak Reexamined

At this point, we have seen a new way to look at money. We understand there are many investment classes, and we have begun to categorize those classes by common characteristics such as High Return, Capital Preservation, and Liquidity. We know that all investments have trade offs, and the best portfolios are mixtures of the investment classes that best match each individual personally. We tend to believe that mixtures of the three general categories provide the best protection in uncertain times.

When we discuss liquidity, it is very important to understand the pitfalls of emotion. In early 2009, a typical headline or business program lead would declare that the next shoe to drop would be commercial real estate. Bad loans and high leverage were the usual reasons. Because of all the publicity, commercial REITs on the stock market were utterly destroyed in the first eight weeks of 2009. Many were down over 50% when the overall market was down 25% at that point. Everyone was panicking about what they heard about commercial real estate and were selling the stock market REITs as fast as they could. Did any of these people who were selling the REITs spend the time to find out how the actual buildings within the REIT were performing? Before they sold, did they find out who the tenants were, how long the leases were, what percentage of the leases was to expire soon, and how many tenants were leaving? Or did they just emotionally sell the shares because that was the only thing they knew to do?

I argue most did the latter.

Non-traded REITs are another form of investment in large commercial real estate. Many of these groups are in the same types of properties that the stock market REITs are in, and the non-traded ones are doing fine. How is it possible that one group does well and the other group does poorly even though they are basically the same thing? The answer generally lies with the liquidity of the investment. The stock market REITs are controlled effectively by the general public and tend to be liquid, whereas the non-traded REITs are controlled by people who manage them as a business and know the status of their tenants, their leases, their occupancy, etc.

If you want to sell your shares in a non-traded REIT, you can redeem them back to the originator of the shares at the market value of the actual buildings. The value, having been determined by the people who bought the buildings, know the leases, the tenants, and in fact know as much as possible about the buildings to determine the NAV, or Net Asset Value. Yes, in non-traded REITs, there is a penalty for withdrawing your funds based on how long you've been invested with them. Yes, if necessary, the sponsor, the official name for the group who bought all the buildings, can even stop redemptions if they feel the investor withdrawals are taking out too much and will hurt the overall portfolio and other fellow investors in the portfolio. Like stock traded REITs, the sponsors can reduce the dividends if they feel it is in the best interest of the portfolio. There are many actions that both types of REITs share in common, but there are other significant reasons the non-traded REITs are performing well now, including access to cash infusions, low debt, long-term debt, and so forth, which distinguish them and will be explained in greater detail later.

Why do I like single-focused professionals controlling my money and not the general public? Carefully chosen professionals tend to be much less emotional in their decisions and make more consistent and informed choices. We hire them for a reason. They understand their investment class very well, and we are going to let them do their job without the interference of the less informed general public, which tends to overreact to the latest headline in the latest paper. The stock market REITs no longer follow the trends of non-correlation with the general stock market. When the market goes up, they tend to go up. When the market goes down, they go down.

I'm sure the managers of stock market REITs know that we are in some of the best times in history to buy large commercial real estate but cannot act on it due to limited resources and falling stock prices. The non-traded REITs, who are actively raising money, do not have this problem. They have access to cash from constant investor inflows and can gobble up deals not seen in forty years. Thus, they are building their portfolios, making them even stronger amidst the chaos.

There will be a more detailed discussion of the different REITs in Chapter 7, but for this discussion, they serve to help distinguish the effects of liquidity on the performance of a portfolio. In general, I do not want the public determining the outcome of my investments. I prefer to hire groups who can invest the money intelligently and not make irrational decisions based on little knowledge of the facts. This does not mean that there are no investors able to understand investments as well as seasoned professionals. As evidenced by the recent market turmoil and credit crunch, many seasoned professionals on Wall Street obviously didn't know, or in my opinion, didn't care what the outcomes of their reckless endeavors would be. In general, someone who has spent a lifetime working in one profession, whether it is real estate or underwater pearl diving, that person will have a knowledge of the subject far superior to the general public. That is the person I want investing my money.

Finally, liquidity is meant for a piece of one's portfolio, but it comes with a price. It is appropriate to meet short-term goals, emergencies, the what if's, as well as providing available funds for investment opportunities found in the future. The price paid for liquidity is being forced to give up either capital preservation or high return. Thus you are forced into either the stock market or CDs.

The next chapter will focus on detailed descriptions of the investment classes, and Chapter 8 will combine the previous chapters to provide a comprehensive understanding of building your own financial blue print.

———

Chapter 7
The Different Legs On the Table

Each investment has unique characteristics, some good and some bad. Like people, some are temperamental and easily influenced by ebbs and flows of the general economy while others just go with the flow, no matter what is happening.

When selecting appropriate investment classes to build the various legs of your financial table, the most important question to ask yourself is what is your temperament? Are you a gambler who likes the excitement of possibly doubling your money in a very short period of time, or do you seek stability, wanting nothing but consistency in your life?

All investments are worth considering, and sometimes having a mixture of the extremes and everything in between is sometimes the answer. The young hotshot looking to double his money may benefit greatly by adding the consistent performing thoroughbreds, and the ninety-five-year-old widow may benefit from adding some inflation busting quarter horses. The bottom line for any portfolio is balance, and from experience, we feel that the portfolios with the most legs or "checks in the mail" are the most successful ones. Let's say you have twenty different legs or sub-legs on your financial table. Maybe check number three drops one month, but check number eight and number fourteen rise that same month. Overall, you are still in the ballpark of what you expected for income that particular month or year, even though some investments have not performed as well as hoped, while others have exceeded your expectations.

The ultimate design of a portfolio will depend on the individual investor's beliefs. If someone has always made their money in real estate and feels this is the only investment class worth its weight in salt, then adding an equipment lease trust or mutual fund probably won't work for them. They do not believe this investment will work and in the future will tend to look for reasons why it is not working, and thus, the bad investment becomes a self-fulfilling prophecy. You're setting yourself up for disappointment by adding investments that don't match your beliefs. You will find the negative.

On the flip side, using investments that match your beliefs will provide you a sense of calm in tumultuous times. I've seen the most loyal stock believers sit back, cool as a cucumber, while their portfolios of stocks and bonds were crashing 40–50%. They absolutely believed in the longevity of their positions, and nothing could rattle them.

One's beliefs tend to be shaped by past experiences. A client came in for a consultation, and the first thing out of his mouth was the time he lost five thousand dollars in an oil/gas exploratory drilling program back in 1987. His previous advisor told him all these reasons for going into the position, such as tax benefits, huge returns, etc., and what happened next? The single well project came in dry, and he got nothing but a five-thousand-dollar tax deduction. Since then, he has always told the story of why oil/gas investments are worthless and scams. I'm sure individuals like Rockefeller would disagree, but that's not the point. For this man, unless he was open to setting aside his opinion formed over the last twenty years, oil/gas investments would most likely not be a good fit.

Time and Real Assets

Many articles written today discuss the impending commercial real estate crash. Vacancies will explode, and these properties will lose half their value. The result has been a slaughtering of stock market REITs, many dropping much more than 50%, as previously described in Chapter 6.

A key to real assets is time and inflation. Let's say you just inherited the Empire State Building from a long lost family billionaire and were informed that the building had no debt on it, had net positive cash flow of a million a month, but was probably not as valuable as it was in 2007 and not a good time to sell, would you feel compelled to sell? Would you feel panic if you sat around collecting rents to the tune of a million a month? Probably not! Over time, the beauty of real assets is that they tend to be worth more eventually. In the meantime, you're enjoying the income from rents. The nice thing about rental rates is that they tend to follow inflation. If the rent would buy one hundred loaves of bread today, then in twenty years, whatever the cost of one hundred loaves of bread is, the rent will usually have adjusted to be the same relative ratio.

Since large commercial real estate tends to be valued based on the income of the property, the value of the building generally goes up if the income has gone up.

If time is not on your side, such as may be the case for many of the stock market REITs that have large debts coming due on properties and with not a loan in sight to save the day, they will need to liquidate.

A key difference between the non-traded REITs and the stock market REITs tends to be access to cash. When the market REITs went public, they raised lots of cash and were able to buy lots of buildings. The problem appears when they use up their initial funds and still wish to buy more properties. They tend to use lots of leverage.

For instance a building costs $100 million, and 80% of the purchase price is financed or debt is assumed on $80 million of the purchase price. In good times, the high leverage will result in great profits. But, in bad times, it works just the opposite. Since the market REITs do not tend to have a lot of cash on hand, a lender evaluating them will consider them a greater risk and will usually give only short-term loans. For instance, on the $80 million loan, maybe a three year fixed loan with a full balloon payment at the end is all they can get. The problem many market REITs are experiencing today is that they are unable to get new financing to pay off the balloon payments and must find other ways to raise the cash. The only other way to raise cash is having a secondary offering of stock, very difficult in these bad markets, or a fire sale on the building or many buildings to pay back the debt. Otherwise, as General Growth Properties experienced in April of 2009, they may have to file for bankruptcy.

Fire sales are never any fun for the seller, but the cash ready buyer will have lots of fun. If your house was worth five hundred thousand today and would reasonably sell for that amount if listed and marketed properly and you had plenty of time, how much do you think it would sell for if you were forced to sell it in the next twenty-four hours? That is, what price would lure someone to snap up your house with a cashier's check the next day? Would the quick sale price be $400,000 or $250,000? The answer usually falls in the 60% range of the fair market value of the house.

If I drive by and see a hundred-thousand-dollar house with a sign out front declaring fire sale, today only, first person with sixty thousand dollars gets it, I will be running to my bank as fast as I can. Not being greedy, the day after I buy it, I list the house for sixty-five thousand dollars and will probably sell it rather quickly. Not bad for a day or two of work. Sixty percent of fair market value is generally the quick sale value of a piece of real estate.

Non-traded REITs generally have time on their side. They tend to follow the rules of low leverage, typically under 50%, and long-term debt, five or ten years or longer, with fixed interest rates. With cash coming in from investors and rents coming in from their properties, they have the other keys to success: cash flow and a piggy bank filled with emergency reserves. All of these factors give these REITs an advantage over the market REITs, and that is time. Time to wait around for the dirt to eventually become worth more. Again, anyone who has owned a home for more than ten or fifteen years knows this is a benefit of owning real assets (your home) and inflation over time.

Direct Participation Programs

One way to put money into tangible assets is through investment programs called direct participation programs (DPPs). Most of the investments within the HR-CP category are DPPs.

When you have a direct investment in tangible or real assets, such as real estate, leased equipment, and energy resources, you own a share of the actual assets of an operating company and may benefit from the assets' value, typically the income they produce.

The most common DPPs are non-traded real estate investment trusts (REITs), equipment leasing corporations, and energy exploration and development limited partnerships.

Investing through a DPP gives you partial ownership of actual physical assets. For example, if you invest in a non-traded REIT, you're a part owner of the real estate holdings of the REIT. If you invest in an equipment leasing corporation, you're part owner of the actual equipment offered for lease by the corporation. And if you invest in an oil development corporation, you're part owner of the corporation's wells and the proceeds of oil sales.

The pooled investment structure of DPPs is sometimes described as a way to provide the average investor with opportunities previously available only to the wealthy. Because you invest as part of a group, you don't need the means to acquire a large percentage stake in the venture or fund your own start-up company to invest in new businesses.

In each case, the sponsors who offer DPPs pool your funds and the funds of other participating investors, typically a thousand or more of them, to make investments they have identified as appropriate to the program's investment goals. The sponsors are responsible for managing the assets of the program as long as it continues to operate and for devising an appropriate strategy for ending it.

The legal structures that provide the foundations for different types of direct investment programs vary. REITs are a special type of corporation. Equipment leasing businesses are structured as limited liability corporations (LLCs). Energy ventures are formed as limited partnerships. In practice, however, the investments behave as limited partnerships, regardless of their differing legal structures.

In brief, a limited partnership has a general partner, in this case the sponsor, who runs the business and a number of limited partners who invest but aren't involved in the partnership's operation or liable for losses beyond their own investment.

Accreditation of Investors
While learning about the different legs on the financial table, you'll notice several disclosures I've included throughout the book.

State suitability and accredited investor rules apply—not suitable for all investors.

As licensed security advisors, many of the investments we discuss in general terms are considered accredited investments. That is, the potential investor needs to meet certain net worth and income requirements to invest in these financial tools.

Working with an experienced advisor will help in the understanding of which investments need what type of requirements and will be appropriate for your financial table.

Accreditation rules generally apply to investments that have limited liquidity or liquidity requirements. The SEC wants to make sure a person has other means besides this particular investment. We fully stand behind the idea of balance and using appropriate vehicles for an investor, but as discussed below, we question the motivation for the rules. No one should ever put all their eggs in one basket. You need money in many different categories to be well diversified: some resources in the High Return-Liquid category, such as stocks, bonds, and mutual funds, and other money in the Capital Preservation-Liquid category, such as the bank. Access to cash is very important for some parts of your money, but as previously mentioned, it is not the Holy Grail for building wealth.

Examples of investments with partial accreditation standards include your typical non-traded REIT or Equipment Lease Trust. These financial tools will generally have a net worth requirement of $150,000 or $250,000 depending on your state where you live. Another way to qualify for this particular investment is to have a net worth of sixty thousand dollars and an income of at least sixty thousand dollars each year. Net worth does include personal residence for some investments, and for others it does not. The particular state you live in will set the accreditation rules, and discussing this with your advisor is imperative to building a successful blue print.

Most oil/gas investments are full accreditation investments, meaning you typically need a net worth of $1 million. This again is based with or without residence, depending on the state where you live. When determining the value of your residence, take the fair market value and subtract any debts on the house. If you have a seven-hundred-thousand-dollar house with two hundred thousand dollars in debt, then use five-hundred-thousand dollars as the value of your home. Add on top of this all investments that are in the stock market, retirement plans, investment properties, and so forth, and this value becomes your net worth.

The other way to qualify for full accreditation is to have an income of over two hundred thousand dollars for the last two years, three hundred thousand dollars if you are married.

Other rules apply for entities such as irrevocable trusts or Limited Liability Corporations (LLCs).

Though adamant about using appropriate tools for any given investor's financial table, I am personally torn by my beliefs of accreditation for investments. I'm torn because Wall Street is the primary driver on investment rules. You could argue that the SEC or Congress should set the rules, but I disagree. Politicians' pockets are lined with Wall Street cash, and Wall Street wants to promote the investments that make them the most money year in and year out. If a particular investment doesn't pay a commission that matches their criteria, then the investment will usually have accreditation standards placed on it and thus limit the ability of advisors to recommend certain ideas.

I'm the first to believe in balance and using many concepts that are right for the individual, but when the rules allow an eighty-year-old to buy as much high tech widget stock as possible, yet limit their ability to add an extremely conservative collateralized note program with equity three times that of the notes and a flawless track record over decades, I start to question the reasons for the accreditation limits. Are they meant to protect the individual from less scrupulous advisors or to protect Wall Street from losing that money to investments that do not bring home the bacon?

It is most important to note that the investments we are discussing are securities registered with the Securities and Exchange Commission (SEC). Any investment can be a private placement or an investment not registered with the SEC, but as licensed advisors, we only represent registered securities. Registered securities must follow the rules for disclosure and come with prospectuses. For instance, a mutual fund is a registered security, and that is why when you purchase one, you receive in the mail that big legal document most people just throw out or use to jump start a nice winter fire. A prospectus is very important because it tells you the information you need to properly evaluate an investment. It includes and discloses the fees, risks, management, and conflicts of interest for that particular investment.

Due diligence is the key to protecting oneself from being caught by a guy like Madoff and his $50 billion Ponzi scheme. Having registered securities provides at least a semi-transparent view of the investment. Nothing is perfect, and I'm sure there are countless examples of registered securities falling through the cracks. A great example was mortgage securities that were pitched to investors as a great alternative to cash in the bank. When the credit crunch hit us in August of 2007, these "Liquid" investments became completely "Illiquid." Yes, they came with prospectuses, but nowhere in the prospectus did they fully disclose the extent to which investments inside the fund could use toxic or esoteric mortgage pools and the risks this truly represented.

One client came to us asking for help with his daughter's marriage. He had placed all the funds needed for the wedding in a mortgage-backed security, which was sold to him by an advisor pitching it as a great alternative to cash earning 1%. "Don't worry; it is as safe as cash," the pitchman said. "Just as liquid, also. You can sell whenever you like, since these are on the stock market!" he was told before buying it. Well, when his daughter's wedding approached and he went to sell the security for the needed proceeds, to his surprise, he was told, "Sorry, no one is buying that security. You'll have to wait."

Our answer to the gentleman was a little more complete, but not much. We discussed the secondary market for the security and that if he did want to sell, he would probably take an 80% or greater loss. We felt this was not the answer and advised against it. The man was stuck with a wedding he had to pay for with credit cards at 17% interest rates. The point is this: just because a security is registered it is not a guarantee that it is a good investment.

Commissions and Fees

All investments have fees and commissions. The particular investment determines which is being paid. In general, when you are in the stock market, you are paying ongoing asset fees. With real assets, in general, you are paying commissions.

If you were to buy an investment rental property, say for one hundred thousand dollars, and you set aside twenty-five thousand dollars for the purchase, this would include the down payment and all initial loan costs, inspections, appraisals, and miscellaneous purchasing expenses. To figure out your net cash flow, for instance, on this example, it was six thousand dollars per year. To figure out your net cash flow, you simply divide six thousand dollars by the value of the property, one hundred thousand dollars, to come to 6% per year.

The net cash flow of six thousand dollars is after all ongoing expenses, such as property management, taxes, and so forth. All investments, one way or another, have ongoing expenses, whether in the stock market or in real assets.

With real assets, not all the money used for the purchase is going to buy the dirt. In the above example, only twenty thousand dollars is going into the ground, the down payment. The other five thousand dollars covers the miscellaneous expenses to acquire the property. You might call these the commissions earned by the various parties involved, such as the appraiser, the home inspector, and the mortgage consultant, to name a few.

When purchasing securities that are part of the High Return-Capital Preservation category, not all of your money goes to buy the dirt or real asset. Commissions are paid to the various people or groups involved, including the real estate or real asset agents, the appraisers, the sponsor, and financial advisors who recommended this investment to you. If you invested one hundred dollars, maybe only ninety dollars is going into the dirt. Your statement, however, will show one hundred dollars as your balance, not ninety dollars, and if the dividend for a particular investment is 7%, you will see seven dollars of dividends paid to you that year. You can compare that to the 6% return you see with the small rental property.

The key to this category is time. The sponsor knows that to earn back the 10% paid as commissions to the various parties, they will need time for the real asset to appreciate above the hundred dollars you put into the investment. The rents from the real assets will cover the dividends, but the appreciation is the only thing that will cover the original costs to get into the investment.

To compare apples to apples with investments and cash flow, on the small rental property, you would actually divide the six thousand dollars of net income by the money you invested, the twenty-five thousand dollars, to get to net cash flow of 24%. That is the beauty of leverage and using other people's money.

Of note, we believe the main reason the larger wire houses will not represent the majority of the investment classes in the High Return-Capital Preservation category is because of the one-time commission aspect. A mutual fund or variable annuity is much more profitable in the long run due to the internal ongoing fees that are paid by the investor each year, whether making money or not. This is compared to a single commission paid on a real asset security investment that might take years to go full cycle, that is, to return the principal and growth back to the investor, not counting the dividends and freeing up the money to be re-invested somewhere else, which then allows the financial advisor to make another commission. It is all about the Benjamins, they like to say.

Different Investment Asset Classes
Reading Strategy: The next section is meant for reference of each asset class. If you wish to stick to the big picture of building your financial table, go to Chapter 8 and refer back as needed.

Static Stocks, Bonds, Mutual Funds
This refers to any stock, bond, mutual fund, or derivative that is held over one year. I call this the "hope and pray" leg of the financial table. The vast majority of investors only know this asset class. This asset class tends to do well in bull markets. Since 2000, however, the problem is that we have been in a bear market, and this secular trend will most likely continue for many years.

This is the asset class that most applies to the classic brokerisms, "Buy and hold," "Dollar Cost Average," and so forth. Since most people know this category well, we won't spend much time on it. We will reiterate a few points from previous chapters for clarification.

As with all investments, you should be aware of the real investment fees. Over time, fees tend to be a factor that makes or breaks a financial tool's long-term performance. If you hold equity positions within a wrap account, be aware of the hidden stuff, which further compounds the issue. If you are pulling income from stock and bond positions, as previously discussed in the leaks chapter, be aware of the long-term effects of sideways markets and how pulling income and fees enhance the losing years and nullify the winning ones.

With bonds, consider that we are at historic lows in 2009, and the only reason rates are where they are is due to the Federal Reserve's quantitative easing program. That is, they are legally printing money to buy Treasury bonds and thus forcing interest rates to artificial lows. Our firm has been issuing sell recommendations on bonds for some time now. Most fervently during December 2008 and January 2009. With the ten-year Treasury's yield pricing around 2%, the thirty-year around 2.6%, we felt we were at the top of the bond market and it was time to sell.

One particular client with a large municipal bond portfolio asked why we would want her to sell now that all her bonds were doing so well and were priced very high. I responded with the old market saying, "Buy low and SELL high." People are used to selling when their stocks and bonds are low and have sustained losses. The losses compel them to take action. Yet they will hesitate to sell at the top, but isn't that the point?

If the Federal Reserve believes printing money is good for the economy, why do they arrest people for counterfeiting? You think they would give them an award! Just a thought. . .

As with any financial concept, it is important to apply common sense in a rational, systematic approach. If one believes interest rates could effectively go below the impossible zero, which they hit in December 2008, then they should stay in their bonds hoping for more gains on the principal.

A reason to stay in bonds in these environments is if you hold short durations that will mature reasonably soon. You should be protected fairly well, unless of course the municipality, corporation, or other debt issuing entity goes bankrupt. As discussed previously, the tax-free benefits of muni-bonds can essentially be replicated with other investments that have tax advantages, such as depreciation or other income deductions, yet respond favorably in rising interest rate environments.

Variable Annuities and Life

Essentially, the same as static accounts except issued by insurance companies and accompanied by more bells and whistles, such as death benefits and income guarantees. The more bells and whistles, generally, the more fees associated with a contract.

With variable contracts, you will have your typical mutual funds called sub-accounts. Many variable contracts use standard funds, which are easily found in Morningstar or other financial research tools. But with most variable contracts, they will use hybrid funds, which are similar in name but impossible to find through a standard search on the internet. You will have to go to the prospectus for the particular variable contract to find what the holdings of the funds are, some performance history, and so forth.

I own a variable universal life contract, mainly for the insurance provisions and loan attributes, and not for the stellar sub-accounts or mutual funds from which I can pick. In order to see how a particular fund has performed over a period in time, I literally have to plot out the sub-account unit values every few days. Forget just pulling up Yahoo Finance and looking at the six-month chart. It is impossible without hand mapping the data points. Most people are not interested in doing this much work to follow their investments.

Most of these contracts are sold with numerous bells and whistles, all for a fee of course.

As described in Chapter 5, "Leaks in the Bucket," knowing all about the various bells and whistles of these variable contracts is important. Make sure, if purchasing one, to listen not only to your advisor, who has a vested interest in your buying it but also to call the insurance company issuing the product. Ask for customer service and inquire as to the various "benefits" in the contract. The service representative will not be earning a commission on your purchase and usually will tell the whole story, the good and bad. I've found that this is usually a good practice no matter what investment product you are purchasing. Call the customer service department and ask lots of questions.

Other than the Guaranteed Growth rider we discussed in the fees section of Chapter 5, another commonly added benefit is the Guaranteed Income rider. This is a benefit that sounds very good on the surface but will usually benefit the insurance company much more than the purchaser.

It may be added to your contract so that, at a point in time, you can annuitize the contract. That means you can start a payment system, which will be based on a value generally equal to your original contract value or more with some guaranteed growth component. With the market having been clipped in half, however, many investors coming to our offices for second opinions have suffered terrible losses in their variable annuities, as most market products have under-performed. In some of these variable contracts though, the guaranteed income rider can work to the investor's advantage. We've seen that it's possible to initiate the payment system on someone's contract who is upside-down more than 50%, begin a payment system that is around 6% or so, and start the process of getting back all their original principal with some to boot. Not the best option, but at least we know they will eventually get their money back. If they stay in the variable annuity without initiating the guaranteed income rider, with the high fees, they will realistically have no means of seeing their original value ever again, unless of course they die.

One client who walked in my door is a good example. In March of 2008, she put $228,000 into a particular variable annuity contract. By April 2009, she had $130,000 left. For her to get back to scratch, she would have to earn 5.78% for the next ten years. Add on top of that a fee of roughly 5% she is paying each year to be in the contract while it is in deferral, and now she has to average almost 11% every year to get back to even. Forget having any growth on her original principal.

The particular variable contract she was in had the guaranteed income rider attached, but there was no provision for required holding time, a big mistake this insurer overlooked when underwriting the contract. This income rider stated she could pull out 107%, her original principal plus growth of 7% for the previous year over a fourteen-year period. Sounds complicated right? A big complaint of these benefit riders is you have to re-read them many times and practically be a member of MENSA before you can comprehend all the rules and requirements. Long story short, by her initiating the payment system immediately, she stands to get all her money back within fourteen years. Now the pressure is on the insurer to perform at least by 6% over that time period, and not her. Good luck Mr. or Ms. Insurer with these bear markets we are in.

The main thing to remember about variable contracts is that they are still tied to the markets and are basically static accounts. Yes, there are features of some contracts that make them very appealing to some people, and for others they make no sense at all. Everyone is different and has different needs. As previously mentioned, I have a variable universal life contract for retirement income purposes. One feature of life insurance that is very appealing is the ability to pull income out of a contract via a loan and not have any tax to report.

For instance, if you contribute one hundred thousand dollars into a life insurance contract, have growth, and now your cash value is approximately two hundred thousand dollars, you have one hundred thousand dollars of taxable growth if you ever surrender the contract. A feature of most life insurance contracts is the ability to borrow from the contract, usually at an effective cost of 0%. Let's say your contract reasonably earns 5% each year. That means each year, on two hundred thousand dollars, you are earning ten thousand dollars.

Most life contracts will allow you to borrow the ten thousand dollars each year from the contract as income, or whatever, and since you took out basically what the contract is earning, the result at the end of the year is neutral. You still have two hundred thousand dollars.

The best part though is that the ten thousand dollars you took out is completely tax-free, since you pulled it out via a loan. That is $833 per month of income you could receive tax-free forever. Even though there is taxable growth inside the contract, you will never pay it. Eventually, when you kick the bucket, the loan that has built up over time will be paid back via the tax-free death benefits. The other thing to know is that there are no IRS age requirements to begin taking the loans. According to my plan, I will begin taking tax-free loans for income starting at age fifty.

This is but one of many ways of structuring income to be protected from income tax. There are dozens of books that spend a great deal of time discussing these insurance strategies. Do a Google search on "income benefits" or "loan benefits of life insurance" to find out more.

Lastly, please remember that the variable contract I own is but one of many different legs on my financial table that will feed my future income needs. I am not depending solely on this one contract to be my future protection, as it is still tied to the markets and my ability to time them.

Adaptive Managed Stocks and Bonds
There are investment managers who take an active role in changing the portfolio throughout the year to adapt to changes in the economy and

the world. The managers we tend to recommend essentially rebuild their portfolios from scratch every quarter and do not have restrictions in terms of which type of equity classes they can use to build the overall portfolio. For instance, they can use bonds, stocks, or commodities. They have the ability to mix and match any of the three equity classes as they see fit. The main criteria for the advisors we hire is that they cannot use leverage, only cash. This eliminates hedge funds.

Please note, not all hedge funds are bad. Many have excellent track records, and some have access to financial vehicles that most people wouldn't believe could exist, for instance, Leveraged Trading Programs. There is a realm of finance beyond what most of us can comprehend. A Leveraged Trading Program is the use of tremendous leverage on a relatively small amount of money. Say $10 million is deposited into a checking account; this then opens up trading programs with ten times that leverage. These groups now have $100 million to play with. They buy bonds from one group at say ninety-four cents per dollar and sell that same day to another group for ninety-seven cents on the dollar. They pocket three cents or $3 million on the trade, a 30% return on their original $10 million investment. Not bad. Now, do this trade twenty times in a year, and *voila,* big bucks. Let's come back to reality for us mere mortals, who will never have access to these types of programs.

Successful investing in the Stock Market requires a significant commitment of time, energy, and attention. While most investors manage their investments part-time, portfolio management or third party management, as it is called, is a means of hiring a team who spend their entire careers researching the markets and managing portfolios.

Most people don't fix their own cars or learn to perform heart surgery. They hire people who spend their lives perfecting these skills. The same can be said for money management.

As an investor, you MUST stay the course to be successful. While returns on stocks and bonds have been very rewarding over the better part of the last century, the majority of investors have not been successful at growing their wealth in the stock and bond markets because of their lack of patience and emotional decisions on when to buy and sell. According to DALBAR, returns of 1.87% and 0.77% for the average Equity investor and Bond investor respectively support this.

Time and time again, we hear, "I bought at the top and sold at the bottom." Emotion and not following a disciplined, systematic approach are the primary reasons most investors fail to match the general stock market indexes.

There have been three major bull markets in the past eighty years, and each one has ended in a bubble. In each case, stocks moved up too far too fast, aided by borrowed money and greed. When the technology bubble burst in the mid 1960s, a long sideways market followed. By late summer of 1982, *TIME* magazine featured an article concluding that the stock market was like a "Roller Coaster to Nowhere." It stated that the Dow Jones Industrial Average was 1000 in early 1966, but only 760 in August of 1982.

With the real possibility that we have entered another extended bear market, lasting fifteen to twenty-five years, which began in 2000, the need for adaptive managers who have demonstrated the ability to perform in sideways markets is crucial.

How do they perform well, you ask?

Within Portfolio Management, fund selection is one of the most important features designed to enhance overall portfolio performance. Once the manager has identified and targeted specific areas of investment opportunity, a proprietary fund selection process takes over. Your specific universe of mutual funds or sub-accounts is analyzed by applying a series of in-depth processes that rate and rank funds and their managers within a particular peer group. As the screens are applied, mediocre funds are eliminated in an attempt to identify only top-performing funds for placement in your portfolio.

Secondly, the manager will perform the daily research and analysis across the broad equity, fixed income, and global markets, with the intention of maintaining the most accurate financial forecast possible. From this analysis or "forecast," the manager will make the investment selection (stocks versus bonds, large cap versus small cap, foreign versus domestic, etc.) and fund selection for your portfolio, as well as monitor and update these selections on an ongoing basis.

Unless you have several hours a day to study the economic universe and constantly select your investments, qualified Portfolio Managers allow for one to place their hard earned money into proven hands and know their money is being carefully reallocated according to prevailing market conditions.

Again, how many times did your investment advisor change your portfolio in the year 2008? How many times did he or she even call you in 2008?

Consumer Grade Real Estate

In general, this includes real estate valued at $10 million or less. This includes residential homes, apartment buildings, as well as small commercial properties. The prices of these properties tend to fluctuate far more than large commercial properties due to the type of buyer. The typical buyer tends to be less sophisticated than a group purchasing say a $100 million property. More emotion is involved, which causes larger increases in good years but more significant drops in bad years.

Look at the real estate market increases during 2003 to 2006. This was primarily a factor of easy credit, commission hungry representatives, and unsophisticated or wide-eyed buyers. A couple shows up to an open house, looks at the beautiful blue pearl granite countertops with the fancy ogee edge, and sees four other couples also drooling over the ogee edgework. Feeling the urgency to place a bid for the five-hundred-thousand-dollar home before someone else snatches it up, and knowing they are pre-qualified up to $750,000, they overbid the house by one hundred thousand dollars, taking the price up to six hundred thousand dollars, with the recommendation of their well seasoned, three-month veteran real estate agent. Thankfully, their stated income, stated asset, negative amortization loan will come through and allow them to afford this great house.

Is the house worth six hundred thousand dollars? Of course not, but that is what they paid due to their emotional tie to the house, which enabled the sale. Had the couple used a more rational financial viewpoint, they would have seen the house down the block with the seventies formica countertops and old kitchen selling for four hundred thousand dollars and realized that with a month and around twenty thousand dollars, they too could have the fancy blue pearl ogee edgework granite countertops, besides having an extra $80,000 to $180,000 saved on the purchase price of the home. This example is similar to the faulty purchase of a car via cash, as described earlier. The financially savvy choice is not always the easy, path of least resistance choice.

One small recommendation when buying a home: consider building it instead of finding the turnkey property. A small secret of wealthy individuals who understand banks and equity is to have the bank fund their down payment. Instead of buying a home for $1 million, ready to move in, the road less traveled is to buy the lot and build from scratch.

The turnkey buyer puts up at least two hundred thousand dollars as a down payment and finances eight hundred thousand dollars. The builder potentially buys an old, beaten down shack on a good lot for five hundred thousand dollars and needs to put down only one hundred thousand dollars. Then with twenty thousand dollars in architecture plans, the builder presents the plans and lot to the bank that wrote the first loan and gets an appraisal for the completed house for $1 million. Just like the turnkey house down the block.

The house costs three hundred thousand dollars to build, bringing the total loans to seven hundred thousand dollars, one hundred thousand dollars less than the turnkey buyer will have to repay with interest. The bottom line, for $120,000 out of pocket, eighty thousand dollars less than the turn key buyer, the builder has the same home, worth $1 million, and $180,000 of sweat equity courtesy of the bank. Maybe that is why so many real estate builders have the nicest houses on your block.

	Turn Key Buyer	Builder Buyer
Purchase Price:	$1,000,000	$500,000 (lot)
Deposit:	$200,000 (cash)	$100,000 (cash)
Loan:	$800,000	$400,000
Plans:	$0	$20,000 (cash)
Building cost:	$0	$300,000 (additional loan)
Property value:	$1,000,000	$1,000,000
Loan or New Loan:	$800,000	$700,000
Equity:	$200,000	$300,000

Rare American Coins and Bullion

Two very significant dates have affected this category. March 1934 and August 1970. The first was when FDR made it illegal to own gold, and which established the cutoff date for rare gold coins. The second of course is the day the world entered by fiat into a currency-credit system. The latter is what has led to the financial debacle we are experiencing today, in 2009.

Whether you believe the dollar is going to come crashing down or that the status quo of the global debt explosion can continue on indefinitely, having real wealth, gold, or other precious bullion is a smart way to protect purchasing power. A well-diversified portfolio will contain at least 10% to 15% of gold or other precious metals. Why gold? Because it has been a foundation of money since the beginning of time. Who believes this? China for one. By mid 2009, China will have more than doubled its gold reserves and is continuing to mine more and more by the day, as well as purchase mines around the world. They realize the massive foreign reserves they hold will need to be offset by something tangible; otherwise, they will be left holding the bag when inflation further destroys their holdings.

There are three easy ways to buy bullion. The first way is to buy gold by buying the stock GLD. This represents the stock ticker for SPDR gold shares trust, which has a stock price that is roughly one-tenth an ounce of gold. The differences in the price from the actual spot price of gold are due to the emotion of the markets. A premium is placed on the stock price when the public is bullish on gold, and a discount is seen when the public is bearish. When you own this stock, you have ownership of physical gold stored in England. Keep one thing in mind. When you own this stock, you do not get the same capital gains rate for taxes as with traditional stocks. All bullion capital gain rates are 28% under current tax law.

The second way to own gold bullion is to use a bank such as www.Everbank. com or www.PerthMint.com to actually buy the gold at a price close to the spot price of gold, plus a small commission, and they can store the gold in either a pooled account or a holding account.

A pooled account is a less expensive way to own gold or silver. Your purchased metal is "pooled" with other investors, saving you from paying storage or maintenance fees. In a holding account, you directly own gold or silver bars and coins with this storage option, which incurs a custodial fee.

The third way to buy gold is through coinage. Whether you are buying American Gold Eagles and Buffalos, Canadian Maple Leafs, or Krugerrands, this gives you something to put in your safe at home. If the dollar goes to zilch, you'll be able to go down to Wal-Mart and buy some milk and cookies. Today, you don't need to bite into coins to make sure they're real; just make sure you purchase from reputable dealers. One thing to keep in mind: commissions can be huge on coins. Make sure you ask exactly what they are charging. Around 10% is the norm, but I've seen groups charging in excess of 30%.

To understand a bit about 1934, U.S. Citizens where exchanging their gold certificates for actual gold due to concerns about the economy. President

Franklin D. Roosevelt, in his first week in office, signed executive orders 6073 and 6102, and the Senate passed the Emergency Banking Act, effectively making it illegal for U.S. Citizens to own gold and changing the price overnight to thirty-five dollars from approximately twenty dollars. Please note that these laws are still on the books, and it's interesting to observe that, on the back of American Gold Eagles, it still says a value of fifty dollars.

Rare Coins

Rare coins that have collectors' value were exempt from the great confiscation and tend to have a higher multiple in protecting against inflation. The key with coins and collecting is the rarity of the coin. Every day, on late night TV or in the papers, you can see ads for buying coins that are ninety-nine dollars or whatever price. Don't waste your time. These coins are not RARE. They are sold in bulk and will probably never have any value other than the metal content. In general, rare coins above five thousand dollars will have much higher multiples at auctions than smaller coins. The key here is to play off the emotion of the auction when you plan on selling them. People tend to pay a lot more for coins that are unique and have a story, or documented provenance.

Keep in mind, again, that your coin dealer is a critical player in this situation. A dealer must have the knowledge and experience to know when are good times to sell. It is easy to buy coins; the trick is knowing the timing of when to sell.

Advantages of Rare Coins as an Investment

The following summarizes some of the main advantages of rare coin investments:

1. Rare coins have historically protected or preserved wealth as strong inflation fighters, particularly in countries where the paper currency has been severely weakened. Any time our paper money is threatened, rare coins can protect wealth much like an investment in gold bullion.
2. Rare coins are currently selling at a steep discount to their 1980s highs, and given the cyclical nature of the rare coin market, may be poised for rapid price appreciation in the near future.
3. The beauty of rare coins can be enjoyed much like any other work of art. They are also a very private form of investment, not subject

to the government scrutiny common to other types of investments held in banks and by brokerage houses.

4. Rare coins are easy to store and are virtually indestructible. They are also insurable. Rare coins represent truly portable wealth, which can be moved from place to place very quickly and easily.

5. With thousands of coin dealers available, selling most quality, rare coins is quite easy, making them a fairly liquid investment.

Guidelines for Rare Coin Investors

The following are basic guidelines for prospective investors in rare coins:

1. Have clear objectives in mind when buying rare coins as an investment. Decide what types of rare coins you should acquire, the total amount you wish to invest in rare coins, and the circumstances under which you will consider selling your coins.

2. Keep in mind that the market for rare coins can be particularly volatile. Further, the difference or "spread" between dealer buy and sell prices is normally much higher than the commissions charged by brokers for equity investments. Consequently, for an investor to sell rare coins at a gain, rare coin prices must appreciate at a higher rate than may be the case for other investments.

3. Only buy rare coins graded and authenticated by the leading independent grading services, whose standards are accepted industry-wide.

4. Buy coins as a long-term investment only. Do not expect short-term profits from rare coin investments. Expect to hold the coins for two to five years or longer.

5. Only buy rare coins that are popular with collectors and are actively traded.

6. Never buy very expensive rare coins by mail-order. When representing coins, the coin dealer's credentials are vital. How long have they been in numismatics? To which associations do they belong, and you can confirm? Do they have experience selling coins at auction, and most importantly, do they have references?

Many collectors have come across a particular coin from time to time and wondered whether they had something of great value in their possession. This feature describes the main factors influencing a coin's value and provides some guidance in obtaining an estimate of such value. Remember, however, that the mere fact that a coin does not have significant monetary value does not mean that it is not interesting or that it should not form part of your collection.

Factors Influencing Value
The value of a particular coin is influenced or determined primarily by the following four factors:

1. Scarcity or rarity is a major determinant of value. As a general rule, the rarer a coin, the more it is worth. Note that rarity has little to do with the age of a coin. Many one-thousand-year-old Chinese coins often sell for no more than a few dollars because there are a lot of them around, whereas a 1913 Liberty Head Nickel may sell for over $1 million because there are only five known specimens in existence.

2. The condition or grade of the coin will influence its value. The better the condition a coin is in, the higher will be its assigned grade, and the more it will be worth. An uncirculated coin that is in flawless mint state condition might be worth hundreds of times more than the same coin in good condition but which has been circulated.

3. Many coins have a bullion value determined by the value of the precious metal it contains. A gold, silver, or platinum coin does not generally sell for much less than its melt value.

4. The demand for the particular coin, or how many collectors want it, will also greatly influence coin values. Some coins that are relatively plentiful may command higher prices than scarcer coins because the former are more popular with collectors. For example, there are over four hundred thousand 1916D dimes in existence, as compared to only about thirty thousand 1798 dimes. However, even though the 1798 dime is much rarer than its 1916D counterpart, the 1916D coin sells for significantly more. This is because many more people collect early twentieth century mercury dimes than dimes from the 1700s.

Determining a Coin's Approximate Value
Accurately and properly identify the coin. Is there a summary page describing the history? How much did the value go up and down during the past cycles, for instance during either the 1979 or 1987 run-ups? Any properly graded coin will come with this information.

Online, you can go to Professional Coin Grading Service at www.PCGS.com. You can find many coins and see scale values at different grades.

A firm we've used and have found to be exceptional is Farmington Rare Valley Coin & Investment Co., in New Hartford, Connecticut. They follow our philosophy of "Education first," a mantra to which any coin dealer you work with should adhere.

Other means to confirm general prices is to look up the coin in a coin catalog to find listed retail selling prices or estimated retail values for your coin. For United States coins, use *A Guide Book of United States Coins* by R.S. Yeoman, commonly called The Red Book by collectors and dealers. It provides retail prices for United States coins. It is available in many public libraries and in major bookstores and coin shops. For world coins, the most widely used guide is a series of volumes called *The Standard Catalog of World Coins* by Krause and Mishler. These volumes are also available in many public libraries.

For more current prices, based on what dealers are actually selling a particular coin for, you should check coin newspapers and magazines or auction sites such as *Coin World, Coin Prices,* or *Teletrade*. These sites provide price guides for many United States coins and some world coins.

Lastly, you should buy coins that have been sealed and bar-coded. An example shown below is from PCGS.

Oil/Gas Investments

State suitability and accredited investor rules apply—not suitable for all investors.

Oil and Natural Gas investments are any type of investment that focuses on the production of petroleum products. These investments can be offshore based, but for most, they are from domestic sources. We feel that sticking within our borders or Canada will eliminate the political risk. Political risk includes the threat to an investment's ownership from someone nationalizing the resource, such as Hugo Chavez did within Venezuela.

Oil and natural gas investments come in three varieties, including everything from Exploratory to Developmental to Royalty programs.

Exploratory – New wells in uncharted areas. In general, these were the majority of the programs in the '80s, which everyone remembers as losing most investors' money. These programs have very low success rates, yet when they hit, they have a large return potential.

Developmental – New or reconditioned wells in existing fields around existing producing wells. Think oil/gas fields with lots of wells already producing, and these programs are putting more straws in the dirt. Common drilling success rates are in the upper 90% range.

Royalty – Buying land with mineral rights and letting the developmental or exploratory drillers do all the hard work. For their hard work, they generally get 75% of the production. Royalty owners sit back and do nothing but collect 25% of the production coming from their lands. This is the most conservative form of energy investment when discussing direct participation programs.

Below is a list of many common questions we have seen over the years with oil/gas direct ownership investments:

Is Investing in Oil and Gas Profitable?
Yes, it can be very profitable. Think about which are the largest companies in the world. Chances are, a good number of these are oil companies. This could mean that they are making big profits.

There are several areas where you can make oil and gas investments, and all of them have profit potential. You will need to determine which areas to get into by analyzing their risks versus their rewards.

The potential rate of return is also a consideration. A rate of return between 25% and 40% is considered great. But, some rates of return can actually be greater than 100%. Of course, many exploratory oil/gas programs return 0%, not counting a tax benefit. Who cares about a tax benefit when you just lost all your money? All programs have the pros and cons and need to be analyzed.

What is your investing goal with oil and gas? This will play a part in determining how profitable it can be because it will affect your choices. You may also want to determine what your desired rate of return is.

One option for investing that will help with your profits is to focus on investing with what are called Independent Operating Companies. One of the benefits of this is that they can help reduce risk by investing in oil companies that are located in several different areas. The companies also tend to share the cost of development, which also can reduce risk.

Investing in the oil and gas industry can be very profitable. But in order to make it as successful as possible, you need to understand your investing options, as well as learn how to analyze the potential risks and benefits.

Top 4 Reasons to Invest in Oil and Gas Ventures
There are several reasons why investing in oil and gas is a good idea.

1. Investors are eligible for tax benefits.
2. Energy is in high demand throughout the world.
3. Financial return potential increases as technology expands.
4. It's a great way to balance your portfolio.

Investing in hard assets, such as oil and gas, is important to avoid the potential volatility of the traditional markets and investments today. Another important quality is the relationship of the dollar to commodities like oil and gas. The further the dollar falls, the more dollars it takes to purchase a barrel of oil. Therefore, commodities tend to be a great inflation hedge.

Tax benefits are one of the most talked about qualities of these types of investments. Below is a basic example of some of the benefits you may realize from investing in an oil and gas program.

According to *Newsweek*, drilling is the very best tax-advantaged investment. Oil and gas investments are generally 100% tax deductible. <u>You can write off</u> 65% to 80% in the first year of certain investments.

The Basic Tax Considerations Involved in an Oil & Gas Investment
1. *Intangible drilling* costs are any costs associated with the drilling prospect that cannot be re-sold. These costs may be deducted against active, passive, or portfolio income in the year incurred. Consult with your tax advisor.
2. *Tangible drilling* costs include all items associated with the drilling of the prospect that can be re-sold, such as tanks, wellhead equipment, etc. These costs may be depreciated over seven years, currently 20% the first year and the balance over the next six years.

3. *Depletion allowance* allows you to receive the first 15%-24% of your
    revenue income tax-free. This means you are paying income taxes
    on only 80% of your well income.

Example of Tax Benefits *(Hypothetical Illustration of $100,000 investment)*
1 UNIT in an oil/gas investment program at $100,000 per unit.
(Note: Units may be purchased in 25% and 50% shares)

$100,000 -$17,500 $82,500	Original Investment in Drilling Working Interest Leasehold Cost & Tangible Drilling Cost **Intangible Drilling Costs**
$82,500 +$3,500 $86,000	1st year deduction for Intangible Drilling Cost 1st year depreciation for Tangible & Leasehold Costs **Total 1st year tax deductions**
x 28% $24,080	(enter your tax bracket. We assume 28% for this example) **Total 1st year cash value of deductions (estimate)**
$100,000 -$24,080 $74,095	Original Investment in Drilling Working Interest 1st year cash savings from tax deductions **After Tax Cash Investment (estimate)**

Risks

- Interests in these types of programs are speculative and involve a
  high degree of risk; investors should be able to bear the complete
  loss of their investment.

- There may be restrictions in transferring the Interests, and some
  Interests are not liquid investments.

- The performance of the investment could be volatile as a result of
  commodity pricing, the depletion nature of oil and gas investments,
  and operation of the oil and gas wells.

- There are a number of significant tax risks and tax issues involved
  with the purchase of energy programs; investors should consult
  their own tax advisors and legal counsel.

- The direct or indirect purchase of oil wells and/or royalties involves significant risks, including market risk and commodity pricing and risks specific to a given oil field.

- Cash distributed to you may constitute a return of your own capital and may be paid from proceeds of the offering.

- Energy programs involve the risk that the mineral production will not provide enough revenue to return the amount of your investment.

- The revenues are directly related to the ability to market gas and oil and to its price, which is volatile and cannot be predicted. If oil and/or gas prices decrease, then your investment return will decrease.

- There is a potential for lack of liquidity or a market for the units.

How is a Standard Oil & Gas Transaction Structured?

1. The Mineral Owner "leases" his/her property to an oil/gas company for development in exchange for a royalty interest, for example 25%.
2. The oil/gas drilling company now owns 100% of the working interests in the lease.
3. The Net Revenue Interest (NRI) in the lease is 75%, (25–100% paid to royalty owner).
4. The 75% NRI is responsible for paying 100% of expenses. Therefore, the higher the NRI, the better the economics of the deal.

Summary: For Every 100 BBLS of Oil

25 BBLS go to Mineral Owners and other Royalty Owners
75 BBLS go to Working Interest Owners

What is the Difference Between Working & Royalty interests?
Working Interests
Cash flow equals revenue minus lease operating expenses (LOEs), capital expenditures, admin and marketing costs, and severance taxes.

- Responsible for all expenses
- Takes active role in development
- Less expensive to acquire than royalty interests due to market availability
- Working Interests programs have the potential to generate payout in three to five years

<u>Royalty Interests</u>
Cash flow equals revenue minus severance taxes

- No expenses/No liabilities
- No role in development
- More expensive to acquire than working interests due to limited market availability

I've Heard U.S. Domestic Production is Heavily Funded by Direct Investments.

1. Major oil companies have gone offshore for bigger paydays.
2. Many onshore players are debt-free Independents with little or no bank backing.
3. Independents raise money through direct investments vehicles to:
   a. Lease additional acreage to secure additional reserves
   b. Access additional reserves through drilling and/or reworks
4. Value Proposition
   a. Investors may receive value with cash flow, ROI, and tax advantages
   b. Independents enjoy funding that promotes additional activity

How Long Before I Receive Income From My Investment?

This depends on the type of investment: Royalty Interest or Drilling Program. The Royalty programs typically will have a two- to four-month window. Payments will start small and progressively build to the final amount, which depends on current Oil/Gas prices. The reason for the buildup is that once the lands (Mineral Rights) are bought, the oil/gas that comes from the ground from that point in time is payable to the new owners. The oil/gas that is currently in the system (pipes, trucks, so forth) is the property of the previous owner.

With a drilling program, the timelines can vary depending on the ability of the sponsor to drill the wells, collect the revenues, and disperse the payments to both the royalty (land) owners and drilling investors. Typically, once a well is drilled, there is a ninety-day lag to receipt of the revenues for that well. Then the payment can be made to the investors. Some drilling programs are designed to generate payments very quickly, in two to four months; others are much longer term of one to three years. Make sure you understand the anticipated timeline for payments before investing in any oil/gas partnership.

How Long are These Investments?

Although some energy-direct investments have seven- to ten-year terms, it's not unusual for these investments to be open-ended. A well produces oil or gas on a diminishing basis over time, but its duration can only be estimated. When the well stops producing, the income stream of the investment ends too. So there is no single event that results in a final cash distribution or capital gain.

What Does "a Barrel of Oil" Mean Anyway?

According to the Energy Information Administration of the U.S. Government, "One barrel (42 gallons) of crude oil, when refined, produces approximately 19.6 gallons of finished motor gasoline, as well as other petroleum products.

One Barrel (42 Gal.) of Oil Yields:

43% Gasoline

21.5% Distillate

11.5% Residual

6.9% Jet Fuel

4.7% Feed Stocks

3.8% Still Gas

3.1% Asphalt

2.6% Coke

2.3% LPG

1.3% Kerosene

1.3% Lubricants

0.67% Misc.

What are the Products and Uses of Petroleum?

There are many ways that petroleum (oil) is used. Oil is refined into useable petroleum products, most of which are used to produce energy.

Other products made from petroleum include: ink, crayons, bubble gum, dishwashing liquids, deodorant, eyeglasses, records, tires, ammonia, and heart valves. From a barrel of oil, 47% is refined into gasoline for use in automobiles; 23% is refined into heating oil and diesel fuel; 18% is refined into other products, which includes petrochemical feedstock such as polypropylene; 4% is refined into propane; 10% is refined into jet fuel; and 3% is refined into asphalt. Percentages equal over 100% because there is approximately a 5% processing gain in refining.

Tax Benefits of Oil/Gas Programs
What are the Oil and Gas Tax incentives from Congress?
The United States is dependent on foreign oil and gas reserves. In order to help minimize this, the United States Congress is devoted to encouraging the use of domestic reserves. To help do this, they offer tax incentives and benefits to people who are investing in oil and gas. These benefits are listed in the official tax codes put out by Congress, which are listed below.

What are the Tax Deductions for Intangible Drilling Costs?
Intangible drilling costs include such expenses as the cost of labor, grease, chemicals, etc. These costs are usually 65–85% of total drilling costs. All of these drilling-related expenses are completely deductible in the first year. The first year is considered to be the year that the investment was first started. (Section 263 of Tax Code)

What are the Tax Deductions for Tangible Drilling Costs?
The tangible costs for drilling consist of the remaining percentage of the total drilling costs and are deductible over seven years. For example, if one hundred thousand dollars is invested, sixty-five thousand to eighty-five thousand dollars will be deducted for intangible deductions, and the rest will be deducted as tangible drilling costs. (Section 263 of Tax Code)

Active Versus Passive Income
The Tax Reform Act of 1986 introduced into the Tax Code the concepts of "Passive" income and "Active" income. The Act prohibits the offsetting of losses from Passive activities against income from Active businesses. The Tax Code specifically states that a Working Interest in an oil and gas well is not a "Passive" Activity; therefore, deductions can be offset against income from active stock trades, business income, salaries, etc. (Section 469(c)(3) of the Tax Code)

Self Employment Tax Exemption Information

This section has to do with the self employment tax exemption and the concept of converting a general partner to a limited partner.

The net income or net loss of the investments is considered "earnings from self employment." It is likely that there will be a loss taken the year that the initial well is drilled. This loss can be used to offset any employment income that was generated.

Once a general partner becomes a limited partner, self employment tax does not apply. It is important to note that the partnership does not carry debt. Once a general partner converts to a limited partner, that means that there should not be any financial consequences. (IRC Section 1402, Rev. Rul. 84-52, 1984-1 C.B. 157)

Tax Exemption for Small Producers

This section relates to the 1990 Tax Act, which allows certain tax advantages (called the Percentage Depletion Allowance) for individuals and smaller companies. This tax benefit exists to encourage their participation in oil and gas.

Who is not eligible:
* Large oil companies
* Petroleum marketers
* Large refiners (more than 50,000 barrels a day)

Alternative Minimum Tax

Prior to the 1992 Tax Act, working interest participants in oil and gas ventures were subject to the normal Alternative Minimum Tax, to the extent that this tax exceeded their regular tax. This Tax Act specifically exempted Intangible Drilling Costs as a Tax Preference Item. "Alternative Minimum Taxable Income" generally consists of adjusted gross income, minus allowable Alternative Minimum Tax itemized deductions, plus the sum of tax preference items and adjustments. "Tax preference items" are preferences existing in the Code to greatly reduce or eliminate regular income taxation. Included within this group are deductions for excess Intangible Drilling and Development Costs and the deduction for depletion allowable for a taxable year over the adjusted basis in the Drilling Acreage and the wells thereon.

Equipment Leases

State investor suitability rules apply—not suitable for all investors.

Leasing offers businesses an alternative to purchasing hard assets vital to the operation of their business, especially items that are extremely expensive or those that become obsolete within a relatively short period of time. An Equipment Leasing Trust gives the investor an opportunity to invest in the operational equipment that a company may need to operate. This type of program creates income from the lease payments, which is paid out to the investor as dividends.

Leasing gives a company greater flexibility by freeing up capital because lease payments are less than purchase payments. A company leasing its operational equipment also has the tax advantages that come with lease payments. Unlike bank loans, lease obligations don't appear as debt on a company's financial statements. This can be helpful, as major debt can make a company less attractive to investors. Additionally, because lease payments are typically less than purchase payments, this frees up capital to be dedicated elsewhere.

Equipment Leasing programs offer an alternative that is not prone to the volatility of the stock market. They are typically an illiquid investment that requires a longer time commitment, but that commitment may potentially provide a platform for greater stability.

What is the Leasing Business?
The terms of a leasing deal are spelled out in a contract signed by the equipment provider, called the **lessor**, and the equipment user, called the **lessee**. The contract generally provides that the leased item will be returned in good condition. Then the lessor either sells it or re-leases it to a different lessee. Some contracts, though, give the lessee an option to purchase the equipment, usually when the lease ends, or to renew at a favorable rate.

Companies lease equipment instead of buying it for several reasons. Capital intensive industries—airlines, utilities, railroads, transit authorities, factories, shipping, and healthcare facilities—may find that purchase prices are prohibitive, even though they need the equipment. Or they may own some of the equipment they need and lease the rest to conserve cash.

Leasing also gives a company greater flexibility in meeting its capital commitments in times when it's difficult to forecast business volume.

Why are These Investments Attractive?
One of the appeals of a direct leasing program is that you and other participants collect a steady stream of rental income from the leased

equipment. In most cases, you also realize additional income from re-leasing or selling the equipment at the end of the lease term.

In addition, you can take advantage of accelerated depreciation and the tax benefit it provides. Usually, you can write off your share of the cost of the equipment at a relatively fast rate, offsetting income you receive in the early years of the program, thus reducing your tax bill. That situation changes, however, as the leases mature and the equipment is sold. While you continue to collect income, an increasingly larger percentage of that income is taxed at your regular rate.

A diversified leasing program can be an attractive investment because it is long-term, and because it's not traded, it can help insulate your portfolio from market volatility. Further, because hard assets underlie the return, investment risk is reduced. In instances where a lessee can't pay, the equipment can be reclaimed and leased again or sold.

Equipment leasing can also serve as a hedge against both inflation and recession. In inflationary periods, the hard assets may sell at a higher price and exceed expected yields. During recessions, companies typically defer new equipment purchases in favor of holding onto leased equipment, so lease renewals may increase. In addition, when interest rates are low, equipment leasing programs may be an attractive substitute for fixed-income securities, though they are likely to be significantly more difficult to liquidate than bonds or other interest-bearing investments.

What Happens in the Beginning of a Leasing Trust?
As the leasing company begins operations, it pools investments from hundreds or thousands of participants and uses the money to buy the equipment it will lease.

When you invest, you generally don't know in advance exactly what equipment the company will be offering. But most equipment leasing DPPs invest in a wide range of equipment types to achieve the greatest possible diversification and limit the risk of concentrating in a limited number of sectors or industries.

I've Never Heard of These Investments. Are they New?
Among the earliest equipment leases were those for Phoenician merchant ships, the first example of the now-common practice of leased transportation equipment. Today, the list includes not only ships but airplanes, trucks, train and subway cars, and buses.

Energy Bonds

Essentially, these are notes collateralized with energy investments and distributions. The common sense idea behind these bonds is they are interest rate positive. That is, when interest rates go up, in general, commodities go up, and thus the energy bonds become more secure. Traditional debt instruments are interest rate negative. That is, when interest rates go up, the bonds' principal goes down.

Energy bonds tend to marry the different types of oil/gas programs together. They will generally include both developmental drilling and reconditioned wells, along with mineral rights royalty land ownership.

Consistency of the payment stream is the main attribute these programs are trying to achieve. Assume a particular energy bond pays a set dividend of 12% per year for a duration of three years. An investor looking for consistent income is purchasing this investment with the desire to receive 1% per month. They are not concerned with how much the wells are making other than that they are producing above the 12% and the note and issuing group will sustain payouts at that rate.

If the wells earn an average of 20% each year, the investor only receives 12%, and effectively, the sponsoring group keeps the difference as their profit. Not all of the excess is profit. Some will be used for additional well or land purchases to further protect the dividend, but in general, everything above the 12% is the sponsor's profit.

The risk with these programs is that energy prices drop so much that the program wells are not earning 12% and the dividend has to be cut or stopped. The risk to principal is that the sponsor does not have the reserves or the assets of the energy bond will not cover the return of the investor's principal. All are factors to consider when purchasing an energy bond.

Institutional Grade Real Estate

State investor suitability rules apply—not suitable for all investors.

This is generally Real Estate valued at $10 million or more, including either single or portfolio properties, Tenant-in-Common, or non-traded REITs. The key to the REITs in this category is that they are NOT on the stock market. The REITs that trade on the stock market are classified as Static Mutual funds. Though they are real estate, since they trade on the markets, they tend to follow the markets in general and lose much of their non-correlation status. Also, the means of raising cash for stock market REITs is very different from the way non-traded REITs raise cash.

A Real Estate Investment Trust (REIT) is a tax designation for a corporation investing in real estate that reduces or eliminates corporate income taxes. In return, REITs are required to distribute 90% of their income to the investor, of which a portion may be taxable. These earnings are distributed to the REIT shareholders as dividends. The REIT structure was designed to provide a vehicle for investment in real estate much as mutual funds provide for investment in stocks. REITs can invest in real estate, mortgages (loans), or both (hybrid). A REIT pools money from investors to purchase real estate investments. A REIT has a management team that is responsible for overseeing the day-to-day operations and ensuring that the corporation is profitable.

The overall goal of a REIT is to manage and build a portfolio of income producing buildings to generate income and appreciation. REITs allow smaller investors to own large, institutional grade income properties. They also allow for geographic and building type diversification.

There are three different types of REITs: Publicly Traded, Public Non-Exchange Traded, and Private. Public traded REITs file with the SEC and trade on one of the national stock exchanges. Private REITs are not available on any exchanges and are not registered with the SEC. We primarily work with Public Non-Exchange Traded REITs that are registered with the SEC but not traded on a national exchange.

Public non-traded REITs typically require a longer time commitment, but are not correlated to the stock market like their publicly traded counterparts. They may provide the investor an opportunity to invest in a type of REIT that is not subject to the volatility of the stock market. As a result, they may potentially be more stable than a Publicly Traded REIT. Because the Public non-traded REIT does not sell on a national exchange, it may be a more illiquid investment. It is important to note that Public non-traded REITs qualify for IRA funds and offer a diversifying alternative to traditional stocks and mutual fund portfolios.

Here are the common questions asked about REITs:

What's the Difference Between TRADED or NON-TRADED?
Most REITs are publicly traded. Their shareholders range from individuals to large institutions, such as pension funds, insurance companies, and

mutual funds. And there's an active secondary market, where REIT shares trade at a discount or premium to—that is, for less than or more than—their **net asset value (NAV)**, or worth on paper.

Non-traded REITs are available to investors who meet certain suitability standards. Here too, the list may include both institutions and individuals. But there is no formal secondary market for these REITs, and shares trade infrequently, though most programs have a mechanism for selling shares to other buyers. These REITs tend to be non-correlated with traditional investments, which means that they don't tend to be affected by the forces that affect other securities, such as changing interest rates or corporate earnings reports.

When REITs are publicly traded, however, they are subject to the pressure of meeting short-term expectations, just as other listed investments are. If these REITs seem to be providing stronger returns than other securities, they may attract added attention and their share price might rise. But if their returns are weaker than those of other securities, they face the risk that investors will sell—even if it means taking a loss—or put pressure on management to make changes.

Because the price fluctuations affecting publicly traded REITs tend to be driven by changing economic conditions rather than changing real estate values, these REITs tend to rise and fall with other equities in the marketplace, rather than providing a hedge against volatility.

Do REITs Pay Income?
REIT income flows to its investors in the form of monthly or quarterly dividends based on rent or mortgage payments from the REIT's investments. Equity REIT dividends often increase as rent payments increase, which can provide a hedge against inflation, though the dividends can drop in a market downturn or if the properties lose value.

If you're retired or you rely on income investments to supplement your annual earnings, REITs can provide a relatively stable cash flow. Similarly, you can use REIT income to fund college expenses or charitable remainder trusts. And, of course, you can use REIT income to make additional investments.

What are the Tax Benefits?
REITs don't have to pay corporate income tax. Instead, they are subject to an IRS rule that requires these corporations to pay out 90% of their taxable

income as dividends. As a result, REITs can provide higher returns than other corporations because they have more cash available for distribution. That, in part, is what makes them attractive investments.

A special benefit of investing in REITs is that you can claim depreciation of real estate assets against your dividend income. As a result, you may not have to pay tax on the income until no depreciation value is left, at some date in the future, when your income tax rate may be lower. Or you may be able to defer payment until the REIT holdings are sold. Then the income is taxed at the lower long-term capital gains rates.

Another advantage of REITs is that they don't generate unrelated business taxable income (UBTI), an important consideration for investors who own these investments in a tax-deferred or tax-exempt account, such as an IRA or 401K, or in a charitable remainder trust. (UBTI results when an otherwise tax-exempt organization realizes any income from a taxable subsidiary.)

Because a REIT does not pay corporate taxes, taxable REIT dividends don't usually qualify for the low rate that applies to most equity dividends, currently a maximum of 15%. Rather, when tax is due, it's at your current rate for regular income, up to 35% at the federal level. Long-term capital gains distributions, on the other hand, are taxed at the lower rate.

How Diversified are REITs?

The majority of REITs own property and often specialize in a particular type of real estate, such as apartment buildings, hotels, shopping centers, self-storage units, office buildings, hospitals and other healthcare facilities, timber, or low-income housing developments. Some equity REITs are geographically focused while others are national.

You can diversify your REIT investments by buying REITs concentrating in different geographic regions, different areas of real estate, or different industries or market sectors.

What Kind of Due Diligence Should I be Doing?

Before you invest in a REIT, you and your advisor should review the quality and depth of the management team and the company's business plan. You'll want to consider the managers' experience in overseeing the types of properties the REIT owns, as well as their experience in the industry, market sector, and geographic region where the REIT does business.

Because so much of a REIT's cash goes to pay dividends, the business needs access to outside sources of capital. Therefore, in evaluating a REIT's business plan, you'll want to consider the provisions it has made for growth, specifically how it plans to raise new money.

The options are:

- The sale of additional shares
- Mortgage debt secured by its real estate assets
- Corporate debt dependent on the company's overall creditworthiness

The REIT's overall debt level is another factor to consider. As the debt level increases, so does the business risk, and hence, the risk to your investment.

You should check to see if a REIT's debt is at the portfolio level or at the individual asset level. Portfolio-level debt can be riskier than asset-specific debt because when debt is linked to a particular asset, the lender doesn't have any recourse beyond that asset if the tenant defaults.

How Do the Surrender Charges Work Within a Non-Traded REIT?
Most non-traded REITs follow the following surrender charge schedule.

From Date of investment (DOI):

DOI to year 1 (day 365)	No access to principal other than dividends
Year 1 to Year 2	7.5% surrender fee
Year 2 to Year 3	5% surrender fee
Year 3 to Year 4	2.5% surrender fee
Year 4 plus	Liquid

Non-traded REITs, at the discretion of their board of advisors, may suspend redemptions in any year. Normally, this does not happen in normal times but only in periods of economic uncertainty, when investors are panicking and trying to sell everything. We have seen the suspension of redemptions in 2009 for a few of the non-traded REITs. When investors pulled out 5% of the total value of the REIT, they shut off the redemptions until January 2010, a cooling off period, so to speak. The board of advisors for a non-traded REIT will not allow panicking investors to force them to take actions in unfavorable times. This is the biggest problem the stock market REITs are facing today, with their beaten down share prices due to investors heavy selling, forcing them to liquidate buildings and thus continuing the downward spiral with their shares even faster.

We look at the surrender charges another way. Even an investor who had an unforeseen event in their life needing money and did not have sufficient liquid reserves to meet the immediate need, if they redeem their shares in a non-traded REIT, depending on how long they have been in the REIT, they still may come out ahead of a typical CD or bond.

For instance, an investor puts ten thousand dollars into a non-traded REIT and needs to pull out the money between year two and year three. This particular REIT pays 7% in dividends.

The investor has earned a combined 14% over the last two years and now must surrender with a 5% penalty.

The net return is 9%, or roughly 4.5% per year. Keep in mind, the investor is giving up something much greater by selling the non-traded REIT before the sponsor has determined it the right time to sell. The appreciation of the buildings, growing inside the REIT, is forfeited by an investor selling early. This can be substantial if the investor has been in the REIT for more than four years and sees it as an easy exit since the surrender penalty is now 0%. The real penalty for leaving early may be internal appreciation of 20% to 30%, which will be realized as soon as the sponsor sells the portfolio.

Co-Ownership Real Estate (CORE)

The Co-Ownership Real Estate (CORE) structure is an increasingly popular choice among real estate investors. Whether you are seeking a replacement property to satisfy a 1031 Tax Deferred Exchange or looking for a suitable "turn-key" passive real estate investment alternative, the CORE structure provides a host of options that should be considered.

CORE investment properties employ a professional asset and onsite property manager, guided by an owner agreement, which sets forth the management of the overall investment as well as the decisions that would require a vote by the property owners.

The CORE structure provides an opportunity for smaller investors to own institutional-grade, class-A real estate, with national credit tenants and professional property management. These types of properties have typically been available only to the larger institutional grade investors like Real Estate Investment Trusts (REITS) and Pension Funds and Life Insurance Companies. CORE Investments offer the same rights and benefits of individual ownership but without the headaches of day-to-day property management.

A CORE Investment strategy combined with a 1031 Tax Deferred Exchange can provide an opportunity for an individual owner to exit one property and step up into multiple properties, thereby diversifying their real estate portfolio by location and property type.

CORE Property Types
- Triple Net (NNN) Lease Properties
- Multi-Family Apartment Communities
- Self Storage Facilities
- National Single Credit Tenants and Franchises
- Multi- and Single-tenant Office Buildings and Corporate Centers
- Industrial Complexes, Warehouses and Manufacturing Facilities
- Retail Shopping Centers and Malls
- Medical Office Buildings
- Hotel and Hospitality Properties
- Restaurant and Food Service Facilities

CORE investment properties are assembled by real estate investment companies referred to as Sponsors. The CORE industry overall has experienced support and growth in recent years. Currently, there are about one hundred different CORE Sponsors who are structuring opportunities. We employ an extensive due diligence process to evaluate each Sponsor according to their track record, management team and expertise, financial strength, property selection, industry access to properties, and essential business relationships (i.e. financing).

Reasons for CORE Ownership:

- Ideal for those who realize the importance of real estate as an investment tool but who are dedicated to a career that may not allow them to dedicate the time required to building a successful real estate portfolio. This type of investment allows a part-time real estate investor to purchase and build a portfolio of properties.

Through the repeated use of the 1031 exchange process, the portfolio can grow tax deferred while providing passive income and tax advantages.

- Eliminates the headaches associated with day-to-day property management. Ideal solution for those rental property owners looking for relief from active property management and the burdens that come with being a landlord.

- For estate planning purposes, the heirs of a CORE investment get a stepped-up basis in the inherited property, thereby wiping out the built up tax liability resulting from one or many prior 1031 Exchanges.

- In some cases, properties that are available for Co-Ownership are institutional grade, class-A properties that typically would not be available to the smaller investor. By pooling funds and aligning with a Sponsor, the smaller investor retains access to properties, management resources, and financing that would not normally be available to them.

- You may be searching to purchase a new investment property outright or looking to trade-up via a 1031 Exchange. A CORE property will allow you to expand your consideration set and offer more opportunities to find property that has a favorable return on investment. Additionally, you may currently own a property with a significant amount of equity but with an income stream that is maxed out. CORE properties may offer a better cash-on-cash return than your current options. Depending on the properties you select, you may have the potential for greater cash flow and/or appreciation, combined with renewed tax benefits.

CORE Risks

A CORE investment is a real estate investment and shares similar risks inherent to the overall asset class of real estate investing. These risks include loss of tenants and rents, possible need for additional capital for unforeseen expenditures, and lack of liquidity or formal secondary market to sell you ownership stake.

1031 Exchange

1031 tax-deferred exchange is one of the most powerful wealth building tools available to U.S. taxpayers. It is the IRS-approved method that allows you to sell an investment property and defer capital gains and depreciation recapture taxes, providing you reinvest 100% of your equity into "like kind" property of equal or greater value.

Any property held for investment purposes or for productive use in a trade or business generally qualifies as "like kind" property for 1031 exchange purposes. A 1031 exchange is also referred to as a tax-free exchange, tax-deferred exchange, tax exchange, or Starker exchange, named for T.J. Starker, an Oregon timber man and Oregon Agricultural College forestry professor who taught my grandfather and who first used this exchange mechanism and won its approval in the courts, including delayed exchanges, in the late 1970s.

To read more about this powerful deferral of taxes on real estate, please see appendix B.

Collateralized Notes
State suitability and accredited investor rules apply—not suitable for all investors.

The types of First Trust Deed Investments we work with are geared toward building a portfolio of many loans, as opposed to investing in individual notes. They are structured as a fund with pooled money from investors. The portfolio provides a collateralized note investment vehicle, which is diversified in an effort to balance risk and provide consistent returns. The types of mortgages that are in the fund are acquired through a proven process, using conservative acquisition criteria. They are hand-picked, first positions only, that can be purchased at a discount, have low Loan-to-Value (LTV) ratios, include borrowers with excellent track records, and a "seasoned" successful payment history.

The fund seeks to provide investors with a high level of monthly income and achieves this by investing in a managed portfolio comprised of Mortgage Notes secured by real estate. These investments are typically not available directly to individual investors. The fund invests in fully collateralized first deeds of trust for residential, commercial, and land mortgages, thereby providing the investors with collateralized hard assets that can be readily liquidated at up to two to three times the actual loan amount.

It is essential to acquire **good notes** with **good collateral**. A *good note* has a solid track record of making payments on time. The borrower has been making the payments on a reliable basis; it must be a "seasoned" note by its successful payment history. This is important because a note is purchased for the payments, not for the collateral. The function of collateral is to secure the principal investment. The function of getting payments each and every month is to receive the interest. A reliable payment stream brings the <u>return</u> on the investment; the collateral guards the <u>principal</u> of the investment. *Good collateral* does not refer so much to the specific secured property as it does to the degree of certainty that the property can be readily converted to cash to prepay the debt.

The fund's acquisition and operation criteria are as follows:

1. Select a note with a good payment history to secure the stream of payments
2. Select a note with a healthy collateral margin to secure the principal investment in the note
3. Buy the note at a discount to secure an attractive yield on the note
4. Monitor the note collections, to assure realizing all the benefits that were negotiated when the note was purchased
5. Share all the benefits with the investors

These, in a nutshell, are debt instruments collateralized by real estate. They can be first, second, or greater positions. As a general rule, our firm never represents anything other than first position notes.

Certificates of Deposit
These are bank instruments that are FDIC insured. Most people know what a CD is. It's a time deposit with a bank. A newer component of this category, which has come out in recent years, is called a structured CD. These are CDs with stock market indexes for determining the growth or interest earned in the CD.

For instance, we will use a five-year structured CD that is tied to the S&P500. If you put one hundred thousand dollars into this CD, it would be protected by FDIC, in case the issuing bank goes kaput. If the S&P500 goes up during those five years, you would get the gains of the market as a percent of the growth, as determined by a formula. If the S&P500 tanks during the five years, you would be handed back your original hundred thousand dollars. Sounds too good to be true, right? Yes, there are drawbacks to these accounts, which have to do with the underlying securities protecting them, namely bonds. These investment vehicles are very similar to Index Fixed Annuities, and those are thoroughly described in Chapter 9.

The biggest issue with structured CDs is if interest rates move up quickly, the formula that determines how much interest you will earn in the CD as a factor of the growth of the SP500 is greatly stunted. You will not earn close to what the market makes in a rising interest rate environment.

Needless to say, these are very complicated investments that are sold as simple concepts. Nothing is simple when it involves complicated formulas tied to bonds that are tied to the markets.

When purchasing these investments, again, do your homework and ask lots of questions. A good question to ask is how these investments would have performed during October 1998 to January 2000. The stock market rose quite a bit during that period, yet many of the structured CDs made paltry returns due to the underlying bonds going down. Again, ask lots of questions.

Cash

"Cash is King," the old saying goes. It gives the holder the power to buy and sell most everything with total freedom. The main problem with cash is the issue of inflation. When you are liquid and you are protected, the trade off of course is you don't earn anything or barely anything on your money. If you stuffed your mattress full of cash twenty years ago and took that money out today, how much purchasing power would you have you lost? If you had stashed away one thousand dollars in a can in 1913, you could only buy around fifty-six equivalent dollars worth of goods and services today. That is, you would have lost over 94% of your purchasing power.

The one point we want to make in this section is very basic. Cash does not have to be denominated in U.S. dollars. If inflation does become a significant problem, commodities will tend to move up in value from a falling dollar, and the currencies of oil exporting countries such as New Zealand and Canada might offer reasonable protection. Most of the citizens of Germany in the Weimer Republic lost everything because they didn't realize the significance of exchanging their Deutsch Marks for any other currency during the hyperinflationary years of 1921 to 1923. The same thing goes for Rubles in Russia during 1998, Mexican pesos in 2002, and so on.

Chapter 8
Building a Strong Financial Table

Up to this point, we have covered the principles of our wealth code. The key to preserving and growing wealth is understanding that the world is a lot bigger than stocks and bonds and that the most successful portfolios are ones which include many asset classes, which work together like an all-star basketball team.

The goal of this chapter is to provide a framework for you to control your own destiny, to build your own financial table. We want to take the mystery out of the planning process and give you a solid foundation for building a blueprint for your investments, which matches your personality and risk tolerances. You can then hand this over to a competent advisor to implement and oversee, knowing the plan truly is in your best interest and not someone else's.

Most people we see at our firm, we describe as rafting down a river. The problem is that this particular river has a very large waterfall at the end. Most people drift down the middle somewhat aimlessly hoping for the best, and of course, we know where this drifting eventually takes them: to retirement and investment results far short of what they had envisioned. The key to this river is to find the small offshoot, the side stream hidden by the brush, and to steer your raft to it and to the end, where you arrive at a nice sandy beach, a restful place where you can have a bountiful picnic with your family, without a care in the world. In order to spot the side river, education is the key. Being able to recognize the alternative pathway is 90% of the battle.

Step One: Know Yourself

I will describe this step from the viewpoint of a financial advisor.

The first rule for any financial advisor is to know the client: his or her goals, background, income, future income needs, expenses, investments, estate planning, insurance and insurance requirements, taxes, college needs, family planning, past disappointments, and so forth.

Without understanding the client and putting down on paper all of the above, and reviewing it frequently, it is impossible to design a good plan. You can't make a bull's eye on an invisible dartboard.

Here is a list of common questions to help fill in the pieces of the puzzle:

General
Age?
Professions, current and past?
Income?
Changes in income anticipated?
Social Security/anticipated at different ages: sixty-two, full benefit age, and seventy?
Pensions?
Other anticipated income sources?
Retirement timeline?
Living Trust/Will/durable power of attorney/health directives?
Tax bracket?
Monthly Living Expenses?
Children?
Children's Financial Needs?
Health insurance?

Real Estate
For each of the properties you have, primary residence, secondary homes, investment properties, or partnerships, fill in the following questions:

Cost basis?
Cost of improvements?
Fair Market Value?
Mortgage Balance(s) and type of mortgage(s)?
Reset date if adjustable mortgage?
Rental Income?
Net rental income as a percent of the equity in the property?
Planning/Willing to sell?
Do you want to pay off the mortgage or never pay off the mortgage and arbitrage the interest rate?
Who manages the property?
If you self-manage, do you like the Terrible T's (Tenants, Toilets, Trash, Termites, Teenagers) that encompass management of the property?

Investments
Retirement accounts?
Active and contributing?
Which accounts are inactive or from an old employer?

Do you want to consolidate the old accounts?

After tax accounts?

Real performance of investment accounts over one-, five-, and ten-year periods, taking into account contributions you've made?

Emergency money?

Life Insurance

What happens if you or your spouse dies? How will the other spouse/children be financially?

Estate tax planning and the use of insurance?

Charitable gifting and estate preservation?

Using leverage via loans when purchasing life insurance?

Estate Planning

Special needs of your family/self?

Goals to accomplish?

Gifting?

Reduction or estate freezing?

Guardians for underage children?

Irrevocable trusts?

Asset Protection (Lawsuit) Planning

Corporations, LLCs?

Ownership versus Control?

Irrevocable trusts?

Domicile of companies?

Finally, a general understanding of the person's background, culture, beliefs, bad experiences, and good experiences will round out the information needed.

Step Two: Liquidity Time Lines

Understanding what lump sum money or future income needs the client has and when is crucial for designing an appropriate portfolio.

Examples would be:

Are you planning to buy more real estate/investments in the future, and will you need deposits or large sums of ready cash?

Education needs?

Health care needs?

Large purchase needs?

Retirement time lines?
Age of client?

Having emergency money is important for those "what if" needs, but as previously mentioned, very few large emergencies ever happen, and keeping money tied up in low returning, liquid savings accounts will end up costing small fortunes in missed opportunities and losses to inflation over time. Three to six months of liquid reserves is a typical safety net. If someone has a lot of cash flow, then safety reserves can be even lower.

Personally, we feel the best safety nets are lines of credit on real estate. If you have a line of credit worth one hundred thousand dollars on your home or investment property, keep the balance at zero. If the "what if" emergency does happen, write a check and pay for it. Then pay back the line of credit as soon as possible. At least you will be able to deduct the interest. In the mean time, while that "what if" emergency is not happening, you don't have money sitting in a savings account earning 2% and losing purchasing power by the day.

The other idea we frequently recommend is the conservative collateralized note programs, which typically have one-year liquidity timeframes. These programs resemble a one-year CD, and once that one year is up, the account is essentially a savings account in terms of liquidity, yet the returns can be significantly higher. These accounts are not FDIC insured but instead are backed by the collateral of the underlying properties. As discussed in Chapter 7, most of these programs are for accredited investors only. If the client is not accredited, the two choices are to keep the emergency cash or have the line of credit.

Varying the timelines of the real asset investments is also a way to keep money available to adapt to whatever comes your way, either a better investment or other opportunities. By designing a portfolio with different maturation dates, money increasingly becomes liquid as time passes. This concept is the same as a CD ladder or bond ladder, but we do it with ownership of tangible investments.

No one knows what the world will look like three or five years from now. Designing a portfolio where 80% of the money will be essentially liquid within those time lines can provide the ability to shift and reallocate resources into more appropriate investment vehicles, if circumstances call for it. For instance, by using the adaptive manger (liquid), collateralized notes program (one year liquid), REITS (three to four years liquid), and possibly other ideas with shorter maturation dates, if the rest of the world stops buying our bonds and demands higher yields for their risk and treasuries go to 15% yields, great. Pull your money out of the investments that will earn less than 15% and move them into treasuries. The ability to adapt is vital for long-term success.

Assuming market interest rates were 15%, how liquid are those muni-bonds you own? For instance, a twenty-year muni-bond paying 5% would have seen its market value of the bond drop by approximately 75%. If you purchased a bond worth one hundred thousand dollars, its market value would be approximately twenty-five thousand dollars. Does this bond provide the owner the ability to adapt to the current market place and inflation? Of course not. The investor is forced to stay in the bond until maturation, twenty years from purchase, if there's any hope of getting the original principal back. In the mean time, you'll be stuck with 5% when the cost of goods and services is climbing 15% each year, effectively losing 10% in purchasing power. Finally, once the original principal is returned, how much has inflation destroyed the original purchasing power of those dollars? Needless to say, we are not fans of bonds, preferred stocks, or most debt instruments in these inflationary times.

A last discussion on liquidity time lines revolves around the use of retirement accounts such as IRAs, 401(k)s (or 201k if yours hasn't done well in the market crash), 403(b)s, 457s, profit sharing plans, and everything else that is treated as a tax deferred retirement plan by the IRS.

If someone is fifty years old and they have an IRA that they do not plan on touching for at least another ten years, does this person really need a lot of liquidity within this IRA? The answer is no. As long as there are plenty of resources outside the IRA that remain liquid and available in times of emergency, liquidity within the IRA becomes a detriment. It forces you to be either in the stock market or in the banks.

If you realize that time is on your side, that you will not be touching the money for a long time, then you have no need for liquidity and can focus your IRA or whatever retirement account you have on financial tools that fall into the High Return-Capital Preservation (HR-CP) category. The drawback to this category is time, but if time is something you have, then you can manage your investments and benefit from a different strategy. The nice part of these investments, the tangible investments, is they usually pay monthly dividends that can be reinvested during the years, and once you hit your magic age of fifty-nine and one-half, you can turn on the income streams and leave the principal alone. Isn't that what retirement accounts were designed to be, slow income payers?

Many clients never want to touch their IRAs or other tax deferred retirement accounts until they are forced to at age seventy and one-half. The good news is the HR-CP investments generally pay far more than 3% in dividends, which is roughly the starting required minimum distribution (RMD) percent at age seventy and one-half, and all you have to do to satisfy your RMD is pay out some dividends for a portion of the year, and then turn the distributions off. Thus, you will not be over withdrawing from your retirement account and paying unnecessary taxes on money not needed.

The one drawback to using tax advantaged investments within an IRA or other tax deferred retirement account is that you do not get the tax depreciation or other deduction benefits. If you believe a certain investment will deliver a solid return and that is all you care about, then the HR-CP investment is a natural fit within a tax deferred, time based account like an IRA.

Part Three: Income Needs

Knowing how much income a person needs as a base amount is the first step of a successful financial plan. We always recommend clients to have as many income streams as possible to help protect against the "black swan" event.

What is a black swan event? Something totally unpredictable and uncontrollable. For instance, you own an apartment building, and a giant meteor from space crashes into it, completely destroying the building and making the land radioactive. That is a far-fetched example, but imagining airplanes crashing into the Twin Towers and causing small buildings down the street to sustain massive damage is also far-fetched, and yet we saw it happen. The small grocery store owner, probably in a thousand years, could never have thought his little business could be wiped out in seconds.

The term "black swan event" comes from a concept. If you studied swans your whole life and every swan you looked at was white, you might conclude that all swans are white. You could spend your whole life looking at millions of white swans and confidently conclude that all swans are white. The problem: one day, someone shows you a *single* black swan, as they have in New Zealand, and your entire life's work and conclusion is wrong. Thus the black swan event.

The sad part with investments is that many people put their full faith in their financial advisors, and their advisors felt that the global credit crunch and stock market and real estate crashes WERE black swan events. This was an advisory opinion of ignorance, or more likely, IGNOREance. Ignoring the obvious signs of excess between 2002 and 2007 and hoping the world could sustain such financial lunacy was common.

The global credit crunch and following stock market crash beginning in August 2007 and continuing into 2009 was not a black swan event. This was totally predictable, as demonstrated by the Bankruptcy Law of October 17, 2005. This law is proof that the lenders and credit card companies as well as Wall Street knew this tidal wave of foreclosures and defaults was coming, and they (the lenders) were designing laws which would give them better protection from people using a Chapter 7 Bankruptcy filing and sending the debt and losses back to the irresponsible lending banks.

In 1993 and 1994, when real estate dropped considerably in value from its previous high in 1989, many people would mail their house keys back to the lender and walk away from their residences, which were worth less than the loans on them. The envelopes received by the lender would rattle, and thus were called "Jingle Mail." Yes, their credit was hurt for the next seven years, but walking away from the upside down home would give these people a chance to rebuild without the burden of the debt. Several clients of ours did have bankruptcies in the early '90s, but since the debt burden was alleviated, they were able to eventually get loans again and build multimillion-dollar estates.

Now, in order to file a Chapter 7 bankruptcy, you need to earn less than the average income in the United States and take six months of credit counseling. For those who earn over the average income, you will only be able to file Chapter 11 Bankruptcy, which effectively keeps the burden of the debt on your shoulders forever. I believe that without the ability to rebuild, our clients who intelligently used bankruptcy to give themselves a second chance would never have been able to rebuild multimillion-dollar estates and become high taxpaying citizens again.

Don't get me wrong. I'm all for responsibility and accountability in handling money. But, what we've seen in the last six years with predatory lenders, shady appraisers, and real estate agents up-selling and overburdening people, getting them into homes they should never have owned in the first place was a major cause of the current financial crisis. Most people are great at their jobs, but most will admit when it comes to mortgages and finance that is not their specialty, and they rely on lenders and agents to be honest and put the needs of the home purchaser above their own pocket book. This was not the case, as evidenced by the record number of people being foreclosed on today.

Back in 2006, my wife and I were purchasing a property with great net cash flow. The loan we were taking out on the property had terms of thirty-year fixed, ten-year interest only. Again, we were looking to hurt the bank by giving as little of the principal to them as possible for as long as possible and allow inflation to eat away our loan. The point of the story is, the mortgage broker we used tried to pull the wool over our eyes for a much larger commission.

He stated the rates he could deliver for us, a quarter point below the rest of the field, were because he was hungry and willing to work for less commission. I'm all for someone trying to earn my business by shaving their fees somewhat. Making 80% of something is better than 100% of nothing. After no documents showed up for a week, I started calling this mortgage broker to confirm the terms of the loan. He even so much as swore on his kid's life that the loan we would get was the one we asked for. The thirty-year fixed, ten-year interest only. Four days before the close of escrow, he finally showed up with the documents. I took one look at the documents and they were not as promised. He brought us a ten-one ARM, that is, a loan fixed for ten years and adjustable afterwards. The other thing was, the loan papers were doctored to reflect an interest rate of 6%, but the payment buried deep in the documents reflected a different interest rate, that of 7.25%. He had intentionally typed the interest rate we were expecting on the front cover to mislead us into a 7.25% loan.

He looked me in the eye after I questioned him on the discrepancies and said, "Oh, there must have been last minute changes by the lender." He knew most people would never scrutinize the documents too deeply, and I'm sure he knew we were under the gun to close escrow or lose our good faith deposit of thirty thousand dollars.

I politely stood up and escorted him to the door saying, "I would rather lose thirty thousand dollars than pay you one dime for your dishonesty."

The point to this story is, if this shady mortgage broker was trying to pull a fast one on a financial advisor well versed in real estate and mortgages, what do you think he got away with in documents prepared for the average Joe, a potential first-time homebuyer who didn't understand mortgages and loans and relied on the broker to be honest and fair?

Peeling Back the Layers of the Onion

Looking deeper into the economic events that have been unfolding during 2009, they say past performance is no indication of future results. Many people believe the past has no meaning in anticipating the future. To question this assumption, take a look at the chart of the 1965–1979 bear market for the SP500.

S&P Composite 1965-1979

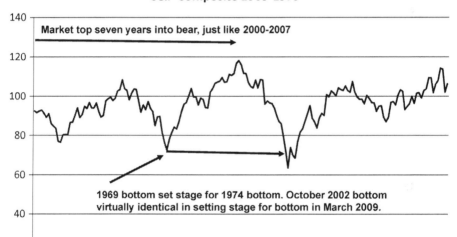

You'll notice that the market drop in 1968–1969 looks eerily similar to the 2000–2002 market drop, and the bottom established in 1969 set the precedence for the 1974 bottom to be down 10% further. The market dropping below the previous low by just a bit is typical of a market blow off, or capitulation, done for the purpose of scaring out the last of the holdouts. After 1969, the market rallied to new highs in 1972, and the financial media was reporting grandiose ideas of future market rallies on the horizon. This was of course only to be followed by the 1972–1974 market crash, which sent the S&P500 down over 50%. That market crash started seven years after the beginning of the bear market in 1965, much the same as the

October 2007 market top was also seven years after the start of the current bear market in 2000.

Just like the past, the financial media was reporting grandiose ideas of DOW 20,000 in October 2007, and of course, when people get too exuberant for something, usually the opposite is about to happen. The market drop between 1972–1974 was almost peak for peak the same as the market drop between 2007–2009. Lastly, the 1974 S&P500 bottom, which was approximately 10% below the 1969 bottom was virtually identical to the March 2009 bottom, which was 10% below the October 2002 bottom. And they say the past is no indication of the future. At least it gives you a head start toward understanding how a group or market will perform if you can see how they did the last time the economy was challenged.

To further elaborate on using information to not be mislead into a false sense of security. All one has to do is look at a mortgage reset chart from Credit Suisse via the IMF to have a clearer understanding that this current debacle we are in will last until at least 2011, not 2009, like most of the talking heads are preaching.

To clarify the chart, each vertical bar represents mortgage interest rate resets in value of the loans.

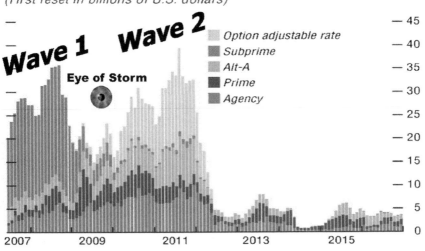

Figure 1.7. Monthly Mortgage Rate Resets
(First reset in billions of U.S. dollars)

Source: Credit Suisse.

The point to remember: When someone's loan resets, typically they don't lose their house until about six months later, after they have missed a few payments and the bank has taken their ninety days to foreclose. The sad part is, in March–April 2009, the first wave of foreclosures was starting to ebb, as noted in the middle of the chart, a sort of eye of the storm. This was a period of false security, a time when most of the financial talking heads were saying we are finally at the bottom of this mess. The frightening reality is, a second wave of foreclosures is going to hit us in late 2009 and extend all the way to the first quarter of 2011. Until these toxic loans are off the books, we cannot have any sense of stability in our economy.

One thing should be very clear, when looking at a chart of the mortgage resets, the second wave is ten times worse than the first wave. Don't be fooled into thinking we are out of the woods just yet. If the first wave of foreclosures sent the DOW from 14,000 down to 6470, or 56%, it stands to reason that the second wave of foreclosures being so much worse than the first wave should have a similar affect. Maybe from DOW 9500 back all the way to 1984 levels of 3500 sometime in early 2011. You think that is impossible? Did you believe when the markets were 14,000, we would see 6470 a mere seventeen months later?!

The next foreclosure wave

Many of the mortgages now in foreclosure were written in 2005 and 2006 with two-and three-year "teaser rates" that then reset to payments borrowers couldn't afford. Another variation - called the "pay option" adjustable mortgage - came with a five-year fuse before it "recasts" to higher payments. Unless these loans are modified to more sustainable terms, they will likely swamp many more homeowners in the next few years.

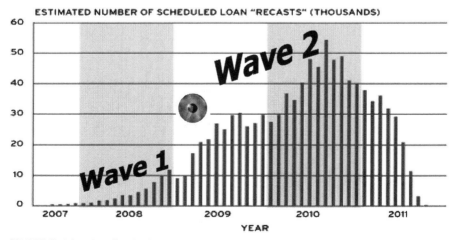

ESTIMATED NUMBER OF SCHEDULED LOAN "RECASTS" (THOUSANDS)

YEAR

SOURCE: First American Core Logic					msnbc.com

To demonstrate how history can give great insight into how a financial product will perform in the future, take a look at the chart of a mutual bond fund or fixed income fund, one you might be interested in purchasing, one that has been given to you as a recommendation from a financial advisor, or one already owned. Look at the performance between October 1998 and January 2000. During this period, Alan Greenspan was raising interest rates, and bonds, preferred stock, and most debt instruments suffered. If a particular bond fund dropped 20% during that short period of interest rate increases, then that is a bond fund that will not perform well in a similar rising interest rate environment and should not be included in your financial mix, unless of course you like losing money. Since interests rate have only one direction they can go, UP, it is time to take action and unwind debt instruments while the getting is good. The old saying sell the top and buy the bottom applies to bonds, and we are most likely at the very top of the bond cycle.

Income Needs as Defined by Cash Flow

As stated previously, a major focus in every type of plan we put together for clients is based on cash flow. Checks in the mail every month from as many sources as possible is the goal. Many of the wealthiest people have built their fortunes from constant passive cash flow.

What does cash flow allow you to do? You can confidently invest in other ideas, knowing the income streams you are receiving cover your bills, and the excess can be used to add to your wealth bucket. The more your bucket grows, the greater your cash flow becomes, and the cycle repeats itself in perpetuity.

A significant part of determining future income needs is compensating for the effects of inflation. A big problem with a payment stream from an annuity is that the check never increases. What might seem like an adequate monthly income today, say three thousand dollars, in twenty years might only buy a ticket to the movies, much less pay for your monthly living expenses.

A serious problem for CD investors when they live off the interest and leave the principal alone is that the principal never grows, and they will start to fall far short of the monthly expenses as time goes on.

Income needs are naturally tied to growth of the portfolio, which is addressed in the next section.

Part Four: Growth Needs
On which conveyance should you travel?

On the highway, cars zoom alone at 65 mph. Next to the highway is a bike path, where bicyclists peddle along at 8–12 mph, and next to the bike path you have a walking trail, where the pace might be a solid 2–4 mph.

Most advisors try to put everyone on the highway, trying to double their money the fastest way possible. They use the stock market exclusively because it does have the possibility of doubling your money very quickly. The problem is, how often do you see accidents on the freeway? Everyone is driving so fast that inevitably someone makes a mistake and hits the guardrail, or another car and causes a big accident. The freeway is shut down for hours.

Funny, those silly bicyclists who just keep peddling along the bike path at a solid 8–12 mph seem to get to work a lot faster most of the time. At least the bicyclists can plan their day with the reasonable assumption that they will get to their destination on time. The freeway is a gamble. Some days, the freeway is the fastest, but sometimes, the freeway takes you three hours longer than expected, and you miss your big meeting and lose that important job. Retirement planning is about reaching goals. Using the freeway is the worst way to plan, yet for the majority of financial advisors, it is the only path they know for guiding clients.

We like consistency with our investments. By using many asset classes, which are not designed to double your money but are meant to work slowly and consistently and to keep up with the ravages of inflation, we choose to travel on the bike path and tend to reach our goals more predictably.

Retirement planning is a lot easier if you use reasonable assumptions and you aim for consistent growth and income. This is impossible with the stock market. You could have saved for forty years in the stock market and planned to retire in 2010, and now what? Many baby boomers are going back to work for another thirty!

Growth does not need to be great, but it needs to be consistent. Singles and doubles to use the baseball analogy. The best part of real asset investments is their direct correlation with inflation. Our government has been on an inflation kick since the creation of the Federal Reserve in 1913, and it doesn't plan to change course anytime soon. Real assets will provide a natural inflation hedge.

Building a portfolio can be thought of as placing money on the various pathways. Some on the highway (stock market), some on the bike path (real assets), and some on the walking path (cash or cash equivalents).

What you are trying to achieve determines which pathway you are on. Most of our clients choose the bike path for the greater share of their wealth, due to its consistency. They want to have reasonable assumptions in place for determining their retirement needs and want to go to sleep at night not wondering about how the stock market is doing today, tomorrow, or frankly ever!

They know they can reasonably achieve 8–12% results, never 50%, never doubling their money in a year, but they can get a consistent total return, and it provides piece of mind.

Achieving Total Return

If you are pulling out income of 6% and reasonably expect a total return of 10%, then your portfolio will slowly creep up by 4% and with more principal to work with each year, there can be more cash flow.

Total Return is income plus growth. Wall Street wants everyone to focus on growth as the major component of total return, but as mentioned earlier, we feel growth tends to be a wildcard.

If your goal was 10% per year, and only 2% was achieved by dividends, you would have to have growth of 8% each year to reach the goal.

If on the other hand, your dividend was 7%, now you would only need growth of 3% to hit your total return goal. Three percent growth seems like a more reasonable assumption than 8%, considering the stock markets haven't earned more than 1.87% for the majority of investors over the last twenty years, according to the DALBAR report.

With real assets, you are usually dealing with rents received, and rents are very closely tied to inflation. How many of you can think of an apartment you once lived in and how your rent went up by 3–4% each year? That is the growth component of the apartment building's total return. By raising the rents year after year, the building's owner is increasing the economic value of the building, or in other words, the growth.

Example with a 10% target total return:
Total Return = Income + Growth

	Total Return	=	Income	+	Growth
Wall Street:	10%	=	2%	+	8%
Tangible Assets:	10%	=	7%	+	3%

If the growth doesn't happen, Wall Street's version of total return has only achieved 20% of the overall goal or 2%. For the tangible assets example, if the growth doesn't happen, you've already achieved 70% of your goal or 7%.

Other than understanding what total return is, you should be rolling your eyes, thinking to yourself, *Everyone says they will make 10% a year*. I agree. That is why education and due diligence are vital. Learn about these other asset classes, form an educated opinion, and build a portfolio based on what you've learned.

Part Five: Beneficiary Needs
Everyone has good kids and bad kids. Not that they are criminals, but they differ in terms of spending habits. Some beneficiaries are great with money. They save, live within their means, and invest wisely. Others live for today. Every dollar that goes into their pocket the next day goes into the latest flat screen television or gadget. They live paycheck to paycheck and will probably work until the day they die.

Ferrari Distribution
A fun term we use at the firm for a lump sum inheritance that lands on a beneficiary's lap all at once is a "Ferrari distribution." They get the dough and the next day blow it on a new Ferrari or whatever frivolous impulse buy they have always wanted. An interesting observation of lotto winners shows that the vast majority spend all their money quickly and are more depressed after winning than before. Most of these winners are depressed because they had a taste of another life and now long for what they no longer can have. Back to buying lotto tickets, I guess.

A great benefit of real assets is their lack of liquidity or difficulty in cashing out quickly. Time and time again, a client dies, and the beneficiaries call wanting all their money in cash as quickly as possible. No consideration for how the money is invested, no consideration for how much it might cost to get out, just give me whatever is left. From observing beneficiaries and their inheritances over the years, I've noted that the longer it takes to pull money out of many real assets, the more time the beneficiaries have to enjoy the monthly distributions, which helps them realize the benefit of taking only the income and not touching the principal. Many parents would love to instill this discipline in their adult children or beneficiaries.

If you have been sold an annuity because it can be used as a stretch IRA and will benefit your kids, we have news for you: Any type of investment can be a stretch IRA, not just annuities, but stocks, bonds, REITs, partnerships, and so forth. The reality is that the day you die, your kids have the choice of whether they take only partial payments over their lifetime (Stretch IRA) or take out all of the money much faster. Most choose the latter. They just want whatever is left after taxes, and they don't care if they lose half the money to Uncle Sam.

Putting Together a Financial Plan

At this point, we are ready to implement a plan. We know as much about the client as we believe we can know. We understand their income needs, portfolio growth needs, as well as what the beneficiaries hope to inherit. Lastly, we know of future liquidity needs or have put into place time lines that we feel are reasonable for having access to the money for other investments, purchases, or income.

To best illustrate putting together a plan, let us use an example. Appendix A includes a few more case samples to better clarify the blue print for the building process.

Case Study: Mrs. Jones

Mrs. Jones is sixty-one years old and is concerned about her retirement. She retires in five years from a job that pays seventy-five thousand dollars per year, and she feels too much of her money is not working and is too exposed to the stock market. At full retirement age, age sixty-six, her Social Security check will be $1,800 per month.

A list of her assets includes:

Personal Residence	Fair Market Value (FMV) $600,000 with a $100,000 30-year fixed mortgage at 5.5%
IRA	$275,000 mostly in mutual funds
CDs	$200,000
Treasury Bonds	$100,000
Net worth including Residence	$1,075,000

When thinking of the different legs on your financial table in the High Return-Capital Preservation (HR-CP) category, a good rule of thumb is never to use more than 10% of investable wealth in any particular financial tool. Investable wealth would be the investments, not counting the personal residence.

For Mrs. Jones, her investable wealth is $575,000 (IRA, CDs, and Treasuries), and thus the maximum for any one non-liquid investment should be around fifty-seven thousand dollars. Rounding up or down a couple of percentage points won't kill anyone.

Investable wealth:

IRA	$275,000
CD	$200,000
Treasuries	$100,000
Total	$575,000

Maximum per financial tool = Investable wealth x 10% = $575K x 10% = $57K

Due to the lack of immediate liquidity with some of the investments in the HR-CP category, it is always a good idea to spread the wealth around as much as possible. You can never go wrong with having even smaller legs on the table, or smaller allocated amounts. For instance, for Mrs. Jones, maybe each non-liquid financial tool becomes only 5% of investable wealth.

The emotional investments, High Return Goal-Liquid (HR-L), and the banking products, Capital Preservation-Liquid (CP-L) can be larger percentages because of their liquidity. You can always sell at any point and raise cash if needed, and thus, the size of these legs can be larger.

Mrs. Jones' Recommendations

Original Position	Amount	Recommended Position	Amount	Asset Class	Liquidity Timeline
IRA	$275,000	Equipment Leasing	$25,000	Equipment Leasing	8-10 Years
		Storage Center REIT	$50,000	Institutional Grade Real Estate	4 Years
		Multifamily Apartment REIT	$50,000	Institutional Grade Real Estate	4 Years
		Energy Bond	$35,000	Oil/Gas	3 Years
		Adaptive Asset Management	$115,000	Stock Market	Liquid

Original Position	Amount	Recommended Position	Amount	Asset Class	Liquidity Timeline
CD's	$200,000	Energy Drilling	$35,000	Oil/Gas	? Years
Treasuries	$100,000	Health Care REIT	$50,000	Institutional Grade Real Estate	4 Years
		30 Year Fixed Notes	$65,000	Collateralized Notes	1 Year
		Adaptive Asset Management	$100,000	Stock Market	Liquid
		3 month CD's staggered in 1 month increments	$50,000	Bank	Liquid

The key to picking investments is to use common sense.

Notice the use of the non-traded REITs. We have chosen to go into three types of real estate, which we feel would do well in times of chaos. Currently, with millions losing their homes to foreclosure, what do these people do next? They sell or put their belongings in storage and move into an apartment. Also, as of 2009, there are more eighteen-year-olds than ever before in the history of the USA. These young adults are moving out of their parents' homes and into their first apartments, which also bodes well for the multifamily REIT. As for the Healthcare REIT, this plays off the fact that there are 79 million baby boomers beginning to retire, and a byproduct of getting older of course can be the need to see a doctor with increasing frequency.

Traditional bonds are not a part of Mrs. Jones portfolio because of the negative outlook for rising interest rates over the next ten to twenty years. The energy bond, however, is a bond backed by oil/gas investments, and when interest rates rise, commodity prices tend to rise, which should make the energy bond more secure.

Equipment leasing investments tend to excel in recessionary times, and the notes program, adaptive management, and CDs were used to provide a well-balanced financial table.

Summary of Recommendations for Mrs. Jones

Oil/Gas Investments	$70,000	~ 12% of investable wealth
Equipment Leasing	$25,000	~ 4%
Non-Traded REITs	$150,000	~ 26%
Collateralized Notes	$65,000	~ 11%
Adaptive Asset Management	$215,000	~ 38%
CDs	$50,000	~ 9%

Summary of Liquid to Illiquid investments

Liquid Investments	$265,000	~ 46% of investable wealth
Illiquid Investments	$310,000	~ 54%

Liquidity Time Line	$ Becoming Liquid	Total Liquid Investments
Liquid Immediately	$265,000	$265,000
Liquid after 1 year	$65,000	$330,000
Liquid after 3 years	$35,000	$365,000
Liquid after 4 years	$150,000	$515,000
Liquid after 8-10 years	$25,000	$540,000
Oil/Gas Annuity Payment	$35,000 Never Liquid	$540,000

Using target dividend assumptions for the various investments, we are able to generate an approximation of her income potential today and in five years, when she plans on retiring.

Investment	Target Income Assumption	Investment Amount	Income Per Year
Oil/gas investments	10%	$70,000	$7,000
Equipment Leasing	8%	$25,000	$2,000
Non-traded REITs	6.5%	$150,000	$9,750
Collateralized Notes	6%	$65,000	$3,900
Adaptive Asset Management	6%	$215,000	$12,900
CDs	3%	$50,000	$1,500
	Average 6.44%	$575,000	$37,050

Adding everything up, the income potential for her portfolio is approximately $37,050 per year or 6.44%. Obviously, the low return on the CDs hurts the overall income potential, but their addition for liquidity needs is important.

Reinvesting the dividends over the next five years grows her account balances to $780,430.

End of Year 1	Year 2	Year 3	Year 4	Year 5
$612,050	$651,466	$693,420	$738,076	$785,608

If we are able to maintain the dividends at 6.44%, her accounts will generate $50,593 per year. Adding her Social Security payments brings her estimated yearly income to $72,193.

$785,608 x 6.44%   = $50,593 per year
Social Security   = $21,600 per year ($1,800 x 12)
Income potential   = $72,193 per year

We like to design plans using only the dividends and not count on any growth. If growth occurs, that would be all gravy on top of the reinvested dividends.

Mrs. Jones liked the fact that almost 90% of the investments would essentially be liquid by the time she retires, and when she does retire, she can easily define how much income she wants from the various investments. If she wants an extra two thousand dollars per month, all she has to do is call us, and we will set up monthly payments to her from the necessary investments to match the two thousand dollars desired. Maybe she does not need extra income but is planning a big European trip in six months and will need ten thousand dollars for the trip. By planning ahead, we can distribute the ten thousand dollars from the dividends into her checking account so that by the time her trip comes around, it is already paid for. At that point, we would turn off the investments, that is, suspend the monthly checks, and begin to reinvest them again.

Having many different financial tools provides a greater sense of control over one's finances and income needs. Of course, the drawback to having many financial tools and legs on your table is that you have many more statements each month. Most of our clients don't seem to mind a bit more paperwork if the goal is to hopefully protect and diversify their wealth more successfully.

A question Mrs. Jones asked us was whether or not to pay off her mortgage balance. After factoring in the tax benefit of her 5.5% fixed mortgage and assuming her tax bracket would stay around 20%, we were able to show her that the net cost of her mortgage was 4.4%.

5.5% Interest − 1.1% (20% Tax deduction of 5.5%) = 4.4% net cost of mortgage.

The simplest answer was showing her that most of her investments would reasonably earn more than 4.4% and that each dollar earned above 4.4% was free money. Factoring inflation into the equation and paying back loans with devalued dollars would boost her net return even more. She saw the logic pretty quickly and looked forward to enjoying the free, excess earnings.

Mortgage arbitrage is the concept of borrowing money at cheap rates, investing it in higher earning investments, and pocketing the spread or difference in earnings.

A mentor once asked me, when addressing the question of whether people should pay off mortgages or use mortgage arbitrage as follows:

He questioned, "Is it ok to pay one thousand dollars for a mortgage payment as long as the money that could be used for paying off the mortgage pays you $1,200 a month?"

Earning an extra two hundred dollars each month for the hassle of writing a check as a mortgage payment seems like a no brainer, doesn't it? For some people, it is a no brainer. For others, of course, the idea of having a house completely paid off has been their goal. Whether to pay off a mortgage or carry a loan is fine depending on a person's circumstances.

This principle behind mortgage arbitrage is exactly how the banks penalize us for keeping deposits in our bank accounts. They pay us practically nothing in interest, yet they get to invest the money in other more profitable endeavors and keep the difference. Funny, when you loan the bank money by putting money into your accounts, they pay you practically nothing in interest, but if you walk into that same bank and ask for a loan, they will charge you lots of interest.

Our philosophy is to be the bank with your mortgage. Pay the bare minimum and invest the difference. The extra earnings are gravy in your pocket. Of course, the key to this concept is having a mortgage with fixed payments. Many people have used adjustable loans for this concept, and as of this writing, the rates are very low. Actually, artificially low is a better way to put it. The Federal Reserve is buying mortgage-backed securities and keeping the market rates down. When the Feds stop buying, rates should skyrocket, and people who are using adjustable mortgages to arbitrage will be hurt by payments that are higher than they are able to earn in other investments. Our recommendation is to use only fixed payment loans for mortgage arbitrage.

One other advantage of a fixed mortgage is that eventually, when you do pay back the loan, you will be paying for it with inflated dollars. I often joke to clients, "On one of my properties there is $1 million in fixed loans. Maybe ten years down the road, I'll put a roll of toilet paper in an envelope, mail it to the lender and pay off my house." We'll call this type of envelope, "Squishy Mail." The lender of course will call it "bankruptcy mail."

This would be due to immense inflation in the USA. The value of the dollar would have to go down so much that a roll of toilet paper becomes valued at $1 million, or the equivalent, to pay off my loans. Though said in jest, unfortunately, hyperinflation has occurred many times in history. In May of 2006, toilet paper cost $417 Zimbabwean dollars. Not per roll mind you, a single two-ply sheet. A roll costs $145,750, or about sixty-nine cents in American currency. In early 2009, that same roll of toilet paper cost $10 billion. Welcome to hyperinflation.

Another story I heard about the effects of hyperinflation is hair-raising: A very wealthy lady who lived in Germany had over $1 million Deutsch Marks in the bank. She went to Switzerland for a trip, caught tuberculosis, and did not return to Germany until 1923. When she got home, she opened two letters from her banker.

The first dated 1920 read, "Mrs. Smith, please come by the bank very soon. I feel we should convert your money into another currency to protect its value."

The second, dated 1922 read, "Mrs. Smith, we are closing your bank account as your balance is too low for us to service it." She noticed on the outside of the envelope, the canceled stamp was valued at $1 million Deutsch Marks. Thankfully, she had real estate, which protected a large portion of her wealth.

The ones who get hurt the worst by inflation are those who lend money at low fixed rates. When they get their money back, its purchasing power isn't worth nearly what it was when they lent it. Again, we'll start a revolution and call it "Squishy mail," and all of us will mail toilet paper to our lenders and pay off our houses.

A second recommendation is important when considering mortgage arbitrage. Only invest dollars in the same asset class as those dollars against which are being borrowed. For instance, real estate (tangible asset) should only be arbitraged against other tangible assets. Often, people borrow money against their homes to invest in the stock market only to lose half of the money. Not a good idea.

Aside from the concept of mortgage arbitrage, there's another concept of wealth that the very rich have mastered. That's the principle of using other people's money to build their personal wealth, which dates back to the origin of money and investing.

Here's a thought. Would you rather have a 401(k) or a 401Condo?

People are told that they should invest diligently into retirement accounts and receive the tax deferral today on current income tax. Wall Street loves most retirement accounts because it gives them control over your wealth and the ability to charge all their fees for managing it. As mentioned previously, who do you think spearheaded all the various retirement programs out there? 401(k)s, 457s, profit sharing plans, 403(b)s: all were promoted and implemented by Wall Street and the insurance industry.

The sad reality is that most people put hard-earned money into 401(k)s, and the only choices they have are mutual funds, with average internal costs approaching 3%. If someone has had money in a 401(k) for over fifteen years, almost half of their account has been robbed by fees.

Most of the financial talking heads and books, which beseech us every day, say to put your money into your 401(k) because you effectively earn 40%. This is the math they use to rationalize it: Assume you divert ten thousand dollars each year from your income into your 401(k), you earn 10% each year, you are in the 20% tax bracket, your investments have no fees and lastly, your employer contributes one thousand dollars.

Investment into 401(k) for the year	$10,000
Earnings at 10%	$1,000
Taxes deferred at 20%	$2,000
Employer Contributions	$1,000
Total at the end of the year	$14,000

It would appear you made 40% on your original $10,000.

Now the disadvantages:
1. You cannot touch the money until you reach the age of fifty-nine and one-half years without Federal penalties.
2. Good luck making 10% each year in the stock market AND not paying fees.
3. Taxes are only deferred. Funds you eventually withdraw will come back out of the account as ordinary income, and thus, you are taxed at your highest marginal bracket. The IRS is rooting for you to invest very wisely because they will get all the taxes owed and a lot more. Notice the IRS put together is "THEIRS."

Let's compare this to an investment in a 401Condo. If we think about cash flow, we know you are already contributing to your 401(k), so instead of that income going into the company plan, what if you took out the income and used it to pay for a mortgage and property taxes for an investment condo? This could be any type of investment real estate.

If we assume a 6% thirty-year fixed mortgage interest rate, with ten thousand dollars to spend, that easily would cover a hundred-thousand-dollar property somewhere. Assume the property will appreciate at 3% each year; you can rent it out for one thousand dollars per month, and property management costs are 10%.

Purchase Condo for $100,000 with down payment of $20,000. I'll address this in a minute. For now, work through the exercise.

Investment (cost) for the year (Mortgage payments and property taxes)	-$10,000
Rent received: $1,000 x 12 months	$12,000
Appreciation: 3% of $100,000	$3,000
Taxes Deferred at 20% (because you can deduct mortgage and property taxes)	$2,000
Management costs	-$1,200
Miscellaneous costs	-$1,000
Total at the end of the year	$4,800

Adding everything up, you realize $4,800 within one year. On the surface that seems far worse than the 401(k)'s $14,000 sum.

The difference in real wealth becomes apparent over time as which scenario is more realistically achieved. Over ten years as you have diligently paid into your 401(k) and hopefully earned 10% per year and if you invest the taxes deferred ($2,000) say at 5%, you will have approximately $216,000 saved.

In the 401Condo, with the eighty thousand mortgage having been paid down to sixty-seven thousand and the property having appreciated to $134,391 at 3% per year. And if you invested the rents ($12,000) say at 5%, you will have approximately $218,000 between 401Condo equity and cash saved.

Here's the good news:
1. You don't have to wait until you are fifty-nine and one-half years of age to sell the property.
2. Taxes on a sale are based on the capital gains rate. Or better yet, do a 1031 exchange into another property and defer the taxes. If you do this until the day you die—we call it, "swap until you

drop"—then the capital gains are eliminated due to a step-up basis of the property at death.

3. You can raise the rents while enjoying depreciation offsets on the income.

4. If you lose your renters, the bills are already paid because of your consistent retirement contributions covering the basic bills, mortgage, and property taxes.

5. It's not hard to realize a 3% annual growth rate on real estate over a period of ten years; most properties will appreciate greater than that.

The point of this example is which situation is realistic for most investors. 401(k)s earning 10% each year in the stock market with no fees being paid or earning 3% each year in real estate appreciation while never increasing the rents. Most investors will probably be more successful with the 401Condo versus the 401(k).

The key to the 401condo is leverage, or using other people's money. You can get loans on real estate. Try going to the bank and getting a loan to invest in mutual funds. Note the bold print above. Appreciation (3% **of $100,000**) is the true meaning of leverage. You are no longer earning appreciation based on the ten-thousand-dollar contributions but on the leveraged/total value of the investment property.

This can be a double-edged sword, of course, and leverage can easily work against you if you bought a property that is a liability and not an asset. Again, a property is an asset as long as it pays for itself and puts money in your pocket each month. We always recommend to clients to only buy properties that have positive cash flow from day one. People have made fortunes from fast appreciation in real estate, but they are also generally the ones you hear about who go bankrupt in bad times.

Clients always ask us how they can come up with the money or cash flow to buy real estate. We look at their 401(k) contributions and point out they already have a negative cash flow being paid each and every month, which we can divert to another investment. Since mortgage interest and property taxes are deductible, they will receive the same tax benefits at the end of the year as if they were still contributing to a 401(k). In the example above, both the ten thousand dollars contributed into the 401(k) and the ten thousand dollars invested in mortgage payments and property taxes are deductible for income tax purposes.

It's appropriate to address the issue of the down payment and to answer other questions you might have. Many people we meet have money tucked away in emergency accounts, CDs, or other after tax investments. They would like to buy real estate but are worried about whether they can get renters. What if the property stays vacant? If you are making the major payments with the contributions you would have put into your 401(k), then who cares if you have renters? You own a piece of dirt, which in the long run will inflate in value. Sure, there might be real estate pull backs, but most will agree, if you have time on your side, real estate is a solid investment and has done far more for building wealth in this country than any 401(k) ever has for the majority of people.

If your job is not very stable or if you don't consistently add money to a 401(k) or other retirement plan, the 401Condo is probably not for you. But for those who contribute religiously to retirement plans, this idea might benefit your wealth bucket.

Summary
The goal of this chapter was to take you through an example of putting together the multitude of financial ideas into a working model. The success of a plan depends on taking into account everything from understanding the background of the client and their goals to their liquidity needs; income and growth targets; as well as having the knowledge, depth, and insight into this turbulent economy we are trying to navigate.

Appendix A includes a variety of other investment plans for different individuals and will give more exposure to building a successful financial table. You will see that everyone is different and no two plans will be the same, yet at the same time, many of the plans follow consistent themes of investment exposure, time lines of liquidity, and balance. Working with an experienced financial advisor is imperative to the process. If your current advisor does not offer these other types of investments, which are needed to build an ASSET class diversified table, you can always call us at Vanclef Financial Group, 800-737-8552, and we will be happy to refer you to someone versed in this philosophy.

Chapter 9
Life Insurance, Annuities, and How They Relate to Your Wealth Code

Life insurance and the various products that come from life insurance companies have always been a great source of debate among financial advisors, as well as the general public. Some call it a necessary evil; others say it is the Holy Grail while still others say it is a complete waste of time and money.

As with everything, no two people will have the same needs, but most of us will need some form of life insurance and/or life insurance products, such as annuities, at some point depending on our situation. Insurance is most certainly a part of successful financial tables when used appropriately. A problem we see consistently is the sale of life insurance products by insurance agents who are not licensed in securities or by insurance representatives who are licensed in securities yet only focus on life insurance products. One-trick ponies we call them. Their answer to all financial questions comes back either to life insurance or annuities, either fixed or variable.

This discussion will serve as a brief opinion on this very complicated basket of financial tools, tools that all too often are sold by representatives and agents who tell only 10% of the story. This is a common problem with the sale of annuities.

There are countless books that cover all aspects of life insurance and the various products, and it is not the focus of this book to dive deeply into this topic but to provide a reference on which to build your understanding.

Why is life insurance part of most everyone's financial journey at some point? Because we all go through similar paths in life in one form or another. We grow up, go to school, find jobs, and eventually, many start families. As we follow our financial road, many check points deem life insurance a vital part of protecting our wealth and our family's financial well-being.

Family liability is generally the first major need of life insurance. If you have young children or a spouse, there will usually become what is called an insurable interest. That is a need for life insurance protection.

Ask yourself a question. If you had the misfortune of being run over by a steamroller tomorrow, what would the financial liabilities and needs of the following be:

1. Spouse
2. Children
3. Other beneficiaries who might depend on your support
4. Your estate and possible tax consequences to your heirs

Family liabilities include everything from income needs to education, health care, etc. If you earn significantly more money than your spouse and you are run over by that steamroller, think of where that would leave your spouse. Besides needing a spatula to get you off the road, your income and future earnings potential will be gone overnight. Will there be money to pay for the bills such as the mortgage and utilities? How will his/her lifestyle be affected? Some would say it's unfortunate but they can go to work. That's one view, but most would probably prefer to leave a spouse with the lifestyle you both had before the accident. The spouse will face many other challenges, and financial hardship doesn't have to be one of them.

What would happen to your children and their future needs? Do you envision them going to college? If yes, then how would they pay for it? If you think they can work, just like you did, then great, more power to you. But if you had financial help going through school from your parents, wouldn't you like to extend the same support to your children?

Life insurance allows you to hedge a bet. The bet is that you will live a long time and it will be totally unnecessary, and thus, some will view it as a waste of money. We believe the smarter way to view it is that it is cheap protection in case the unthinkable happens. By the way, I use silly examples of death as being run over by a steamroller because one day I was discussing with a client the future issue of death and said, "Let's say you get hit by a truck."

The client's face dropped and he said, "My dad was hit and killed by a truck."

Needless to say, after I pulled my foot out of my mouth, I have never used a real life situation like getting hit by a truck ever again. In case someone's loved one WAS actually run over by a steamroller, the shear amazement of that form of meeting your maker, I hope, would outweigh the foot in mouth disease.

All forms of insurance are hedges against a bet that something bad will happen, and the current price you pay will be small compared to the future value. For instance, you have a heart attack and need heart surgery. Isn't the five-thousand-dollar deductible better than the $1 million in hospital bills?

Estate Planning uses life insurance for the very reason that it is cheap money. Many people who have built sizable estates are facing a dilemma with the estate tax, also commonly known as the death tax. We will all kick the bucket at some point, and if we have estate tax consequences, life insurance can be a real blessing.

For instance, if you have a $10 million estate and, as of 2011 with current laws on the books, the exemption is only $1 million, what would your estate tax liability be? In this scenario, $9 million is in excess and will be taxed at roughly 50% nine months after death. How's that for a parting shot from this planet? Thanks for building a great estate and paying all your tax along the way. For one last congratulatory pat on the back, please send us $4.5 million. Where will the money come from?

Will your beneficiaries have the cash, will they need to sell real estate or other investments at fire sale prices, or will they have to borrow the money and pay interest over many years?

The answer to this question is based on the actual cost of money. Bottom line, insurance is the cheapest form of money. There are four ways you can pay for Federal Estate Taxes, which can run as high as 55% on the portion of the estate that is over the exempt amount. Currently, the exempt amount for 2009 is $3.5 million per person, but remember that in 2011 it will revert back to $1 million.

The four ways to pay for estate taxes are as follows:
1. Using liquid assets (Money Market, Savings, Checking)
2. Using illiquid assets (Real Estate, Art, antiques or jewelry, home furnishings, cars, etc.)
3. Borrowing the funds
4. Adding Life Insurance

Here are the costs of each choice:

1. Use of Liquid Assets

The cost of using liquid assets is generally one dollar for each dollar paid in taxes. Since these assets are being held in easily accessible forms (checking, money market or savings), the problem is they are only making around 1% interest.

The additional cost is lost opportunity. If you are making only 1%, the difference over ten years could be hundreds of thousands of dollars, i.e.
- $1 million at 1% for 10 years = roughly $104,000 interest earned.
- $1 million at 7% for 10 years = $1M interest earned.

The lost opportunity is the difference, which is nine hundred thousand dollars in this case.
Therefore, the cost was actually two dollars for each dollar paid in taxes. But for now, let's not count opportunity cost.

- Cost = $1 for each $1 paid in taxes

2. Forced Sale of Assets

There are two faces to forced estate sales: the Buyers who are happy they are getting such great deals and the Sellers who are losing heirlooms at pennies on the dollar to raise cash for taxes due in nine months. Selling real estate or long-term bonds or stocks at depressed values is another big problem.

Most forced sales result in fifty to seventy cents on the dollar raised. For instance, selling a piece of real estate in a quick sale may only bring in 70% of the fair market value of the property. Let's use upper estimate of seventy cents on the dollar.

- Cost = $1.30 for each $1 paid in taxes

3. Borrow Funds

Paying long-term interest escalates the true cost of the estate settlement. Suppose you borrow five hundred thousand dollars at 7% interest for ten years. The actual cost is repayment of five hundred thousand dollars, plus an additional two hundred thousand dollars in interest. A total of seven hundred thousand dollars paid.

- Cost = $1.40 for each $1 paid in taxes

4. Life Insurance

Life insurance is the best way to leverage your dollars. Usually, for each twenty to thirty cents invested, you will receive one dollar in return. The life insurance is not part of the estate; it is therefore free from federal and state estate taxes. As an added bonus, the premiums you pay for life insurance reduce the estate by like amounts and therefore further reduce the portion of the estate that is taxable.

Please note that life insurance must be part of a more comprehensive Trust arrangement, which allows it to be excluded from your estate. If you purchase a life policy and you are the owner, instead of placing it in a special IRS exempt trust, the death benefits will be included in your estate and will also be subject to tax. When you set up these life policies, you must insist on setting up all necessary parts and not cutting any corners.

Many insurance agents love to sell estate tax policies because they are generally very large. The problem occurs when an agent focuses on the sale and is not well versed in estate planning and does not want to include an estate planning attorney in the process. In fear of complicating the sale, he or she may skip necessary steps, such as an Irrevocable Life Insurance Trust, to speed up the time to receive their payday. This probably sounds like the opinion of someone who is very jaded. We are. We have seen countless examples of people who were sold a life policy and had the right idea, but due to an incomplete process on the part of the sales person, the client's situation was not protected and was left vulnerable and little improved.

The bottom line using life insurance is that estate liabilities are paid FOR the estate but not FROM the estate! The estate receives the funds it requires to meet its liabilities, and the estate beneficiaries receive their full inheritance, undiminished in any way.

- Cost = $0.20 to $0.30 for each $1 paid in taxes

The order of importance when designing your estate plan should always be:
1. Attorney
2. CPA
3. Life insurance

The goal is to reduce your estate tax liability as much as possible via trust and accounting work. The taxes that are left, after reducing them with the first two estate planning priorities, use life insurance to cover. This is not a popular belief among insurance agents because using this priority system will effectively cut down their commission drastically and save you a lot of money each year in lower insurance premiums.

Annuities

Life insurance is the financial tool that protects you from living too short. Annuities are the life insurance tool for protecting you from living too long. Anyone who has retired from a company and is being paid a monthly check has an annuity. The annuity was purchased by your previous employer from the pension funds available for your retirement, and now you have your monthly check.

Most people know of annuities as forever investments, a payout that stops the day you die, leaving nothing to your beneficiaries. Though this is one path you can take with annuities, most people use them as tax deferred savings, vehicles that work similar to a CD. You save your money, it grows, and eventually, the CD or annuity matures and you can withdraw your money and move it somewhere else. The annuitization features can be implemented, or they may never be used. Annuitization means converting the annuity policy from a deferred-savings vehicle to an income-paying vehicle. You can pick from different periods for the payout to continue, from five, ten, to fifteen or more year increments for various life payout options.

Again, this book is not intended to teach everything about annuities and life insurance, as there are hundreds of others you can easily pick up at your local bookstore or library or go online to further your education. Some useful titles would be:

- Questions and Answers on Life Insurance: The Life Insurance Toolbook by Anthony Steuer

- The Truth About Buying Annuities by Steve Weisman

This chapter is intended to give you our opinion from personal experience and hopefully introduce you to some of the little-known features of annuities, which few if any insurance representatives will share with a client before they buy.

Index Universal Life and Index Fixed Annuities

These versions of universal life (UL) and fixed annuities (FA) have the ability to earn interest based on common indexes such as the S&P500, the

NASDAQ 100, or others. They are sold as the ideal product. They will make money for you if the stock market goes up, and they will protect your principal if the stock market goes down. Sounds like the ultimate investment vehicle.

The single biggest problem we see with these financial tools is the ability of the insurance company issuing the products to change the way they calculate the interest. To explain in more detail, each Index UL and Index FA has different means of calculating what interest you earn each year based on the various stock market indexes.

We like to describe the different means of calculating interest as engines in a car. Imagine you have a garage with four cars, maybe all Toyota Camrys. From the outside, they appear exactly the same, but on the inside, each car has a different type of engine. One has an electric motor, one has a V6, one a V8, and one has the turbo edition. Each engine will perform differently under different road conditions.

One of the engines in Index UL and FA is called the participation rate. Again, this is a method of calculating the interest that a particular UL or FA will earn based on an index such as the S&P500.

Assume an annuity has a participation rate of 80% of the S&P500. On the anniversary of your Index UL or FA, they will record the value of the S&P500. On the next anniversary, they will record the value of the S&P500, calculate the return, say the markets rose 10%, and then apply the participation rate, 80%, to the market gains and you have a total return for the annuity of 8%.

Market gains x Participation Rate = Index credit for that year

10 x 80% = 8

This 8% interest rate is then applied to your annuity contract value for that year. If you have an annuity starting at one hundred thousand dollars and you gain 8%, your new contract value is $108,000 for the next year. This value can never drop due to poor market conditions in the future; it is locked in! Sounds good so far, right?

This is usually where the story ends when most insurance agents sell these products. The problem, buried in the Index UL or FA contract, is that the insurance company says it has the ability to change the participation rate on each contract anniversary at its discretion. Sort of like changing the governor on an engine. A governor is a device that limits the performance or top speed of a car's engine. A particular BMW might be able to drive 175 mph, but the manufacturer puts a governor on the engine to limit it to a maximum speed of 125 mph.

Insurance companies have the ability to change the settings on the governors they placed on their Index UL policies and Index FA policies on each anniversary. The reason they do this is to limit the upside potential of the contract, and frankly, keep the difference.

Agents will say the companies will not do this because it would not be good for the clients and thus, not good for them, but in our experience, this means nothing.

More often than not, the first year in these contracts, the engines are set for full power. It makes them easy to sell. But once you have purchased a particular Index UL or FA, and are committed to the policy for five, ten, or fifteen years or longer, with high surrender charges for canceling the contract early, we have seen virtually every insurance carrier crank down the governors so much that the up-side potential of the policies is almost insignificant in most normal stock market years.

For one particular Index FA, we saw the insurance company set the governors on the contract so low that if the S&P500 rose 30% in a year, this contract might earn 4.5%. The insurance company keeps the difference. Sounds like Wall Street, doesn't it?

Other crediting methods or engines in Index UL or FAs are called Spread Fees and Cap Rates. The engines are usually mixtures of these three methods of calculating the rate of return of an index like the S&P500.

Before buying one of these Index UL or FAs, find out the minimum rates to which these methods can be reduced. Ask for a history from the company on existing policies. There are a few companies that have maintained an honorable co-existence with their policy owners. That is, the insurance company has kept its side of the bargain and has not lowered rates very much, if anything at all.

Why is it important to have some upside potential with an Index UL or FA? Sure, your principal is protected in bad years, but in good years, if you are not making anything, you basically go sideways or barely up, and inflation will eat you alive. This is why we do not include these products on the teeter-totter because they don't really match the three main asset categories. According to the rule that you only have to give up one of three descriptors, High Return or Capital Preservation or Liquidity, Index UL and FAs really are only Capital Preservation. They are not liquid and will not achieve the high return goal. You give up two of the three descriptions.

In our opinion, variable annuities do not qualify for any of the three descriptions. Due to the high fees, it is very difficult to maintain a high return. They are not liquid in general, and they do not provide capital preservation during your life. If you die and have the death benefit attached, they will protect your principal, but who wants a benefit you have to die to get?

You might ask who then benefits from a variable annuity? Two groups come to mind: the agent selling them, of course, and the insurance company!

MVA Versus Non-MVA Annuities and Why You Need to Know This
The second important piece of advice to ask concerning Index UL and FAs, is whether a contract is an MVA contract or not.

MVA stands for Market Value Adjustment and is a feature that affects the surrender value of a policy. Since all annuities and life policies are bond based, they are affected by fluctuating market interest rates.

The surrender value is the amount you could walk away with if you decided to cancel the policy early.

For instance, let's imagine you put one hundred thousand dollars into an FA that has a surrender fee of 10% the first three years. If you walk away after the first year, assuming no growth, the most they would give you is ninety thousand dollars. You are breaking the contract early, and that is the penalty.

In an MVA policy, the surrender value is based on current market interest rates, which are compared to the rate when you got in. Right now, rates are at all time lows. If interest rates take off and rise 3–5%, you will see the surrender value in an MVA policy fall like a rock.

For instance, in the above example, if market interest rates rise 5%, the surrender value might drop from ninety thousand to fifty thousand dollars. Even though the contract says 10% surrender charge, this of course is based on interest rates staying the same during the three years. If you need to take your money out, you will not be handed ninety thousand dollars. Instead, the surrender value will come to fifty thousand dollars.

In non-MVA contracts, the surrender value is not based on the rising and falling interest rate tide. If the contract says 10% surrender charge, then the surrender value will be 10% less than the full contract value.

Final Thoughts

Life insurance and annuities serve a purpose and can be vital parts of a well-rounded financial table. From family liabilities and estate taxes to the need for another pension or CD-like investment, the most important tip when buying insurance products or any investment for that matter is to ask questions. Every financial situation is different and determines the solution necessary. There are no investments that are always bad or always good; it depends on each client and their personal situations. From the gentleman who loves watching unaware ATM users looking at his $1 million checking account balance, to the doctor with the 401(k), which after close inspection had lost money over the last fifteen years. Each situation is different, and that is the job of your financial advisor to help guide you through the twists and turns of the financial maze.

———

Conclusion
Time to Take Action!

Many people are driving around with broken portfolios, just as some people drive around with slipping clutches in their cars. We hire mechanics to fix our cars, and if they don't, we either have them redo their work or find a new mechanic. You should not accept a financial advisor who has a bury-your-head-in-the-sand approach to investments and your estate. Considering the years ahead and the turmoil we have yet to experience, doing nothing is doing something. You are admitting defeat, or worse, accepting the fact that you have lost a lot of money and there is nothing you can do about it except wait for things to improve.

Did the passengers of the U.S. Airways plane that came down in the Hudson River give up and wait it out? Of course not? One would reasonably agree that crash landing a passenger plane is about as bad and unfortunately lethal as it gets. But, when they hit the water and came to rest, instead of thinking that it was hopeless, admitting defeat, and remaining in their seats hoping for rescue, the passengers immediately crawled out the exits and onto the wings and stepped into the waiting boats in an orderly fashion. They chose to alter their futures and survive, in light of what most would expect would be the outcome of being on a plane forced to make a crash landing. If someone had chosen to wait inside the plane, we all know what happened next. The plane eventually sank.

If you have a broken wealth bucket, as the passengers had a broken plane, you can choose to alter your financial future. With the understanding of building financial tables and using as many asset classes or legs as possible, no matter what comes our way in the future, you will stand a better chance of protecting your wealth, plugging the holes in your bucket, and growing your financial security.

No one knows the future. We might greatly improve from this point, go sideways, or fall even further into despair.

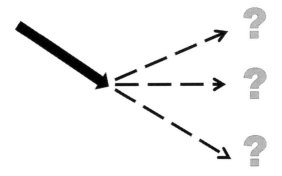

The main reason to reassess your financial table is to lower your exposure to categories that don't match your financial goals and strengthen your table by increasing your coverage in other asset classes to truly diversify. Of the three possible scenarios for the future, an asset class diversified table can reasonably eliminate the worst of the three economic outcomes.

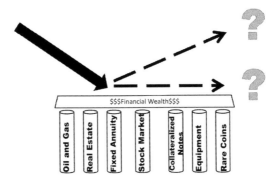

According to *Wikipedia, The Free Encyclopedia*, dated 9 April 2009, "common sense" is defined in the following way:

> *What most people would consider prudent and of sound judgment, without reliance on esoteric knowledge or study or research, but based upon what they see as knowledge held by people "in common." Thus "common sense" equates to the knowledge and experience which most people allegedly have, or which the person using the term believes that they do or should have.*

The most important guiding principle when building your financial table is the use of common sense, along with your newfound "Uncommon Knowledge." The investments we have discussed in this book have strengths and weaknesses, and most certainly will work for some people but for others might be completely unacceptable as part of their financial plan. The goal has been to provide a more complete framework for you to take control of your financial destiny.

The key to everything is education, and successful wealth building can be accomplished by gaining enough of an understanding of finance to navigate and overcome the challenges along the way. If life were a placid lake where you could get from Point A to Point B without a single ripple affecting your crossing, there would be no need for guides or mentors. We all know this is not the case. Life is more like a turbulent Class 5 rapid through the Grand Canyon, with rocks and trees in our pathway. Hopefully, this book has provided a new guide for the back of your raft, to help you steer around unforeseen obstacles and provide a new foundation or perspective on which to build your own strong financial table.

Appendix A

The following are additional examples of building a strong financial table using our methodology of asset class diversification. Please note that these examples are based on the individual circumstances of each investor. They are not meant to be blanket recommendations and are for educational purposes only. Please consult with your financial advisor, or feel free to call us at Vanclef Financial Group, 800-737-8552, or go to our website www. VFGroup.net for more information.

Mr. Johnson

Mr. Johnson is seventy-eight years old and concerned about his income. He is living off his social security checks and doesn't like to touch his stock portfolio because he never knows when it is a good time to sell. He would like more income from dividends yet feels the dividends from most stocks are too low and will not keep up with rising costs.

After analyzing his stocks and mutual funds, he realizes he hasn't made a dime in the last ten years. His portfolio has followed the markets up and down, like the majority of investors with similar portfolios. If he were to sell anything, there would only be a small amount of capital gains tax due on a few of his older stock positions and nothing on his mutual funds. Because the cost basis for mutual funds increases each year with each taxable dividend, his basis now exceeds the current market value of the funds and no taxes would be due.

Lastly, he feels he might have some health issues and wants to keep a fair amount of his after-tax money liquid for emergencies.

A list of his assets includes:

Personal Residence	Fair Market Value (FMV) $400,000 and paid off
IRA	$50,000 mostly in mutual funds
After tax Stock and Mutual Funds	$300,000
CDs	$50,000
Net worth including Residence	$800,000

Investable wealth:

IRA	$50,000
After tax Stock and Mutual Funds	$300,000
CD	$50,000
Total	$400,000

Maximum per Real Asset financial investment:
Investable Wealth x 10% = $400K x 10% = $40K

Designing Mr. Johnson's plan was based on several criteria.

First, he is only partially accredited, which means he is not allowed to invest in financial tools such as collateralized notes or oil/gas programs, per SEC guidelines.

The investments available to him include a fixed annuity, banking products, non-traded REITs, equipment leases, and adaptive management. Of course, we could add variable annuities and static stocks and bonds, but we tend to avoid these categories for most of our clients due to a poor outlook going forward.

Liquidity is important, and considering that he is seventy-eight years old, we stuck to investments with durations of no more than four years. The equipment leasing category is excluded due to longer maturation dates of eight years or more. We choose to leave his CD's alone, sacrificing return for liquidity.

Although fixed annuities do not normally play a part in plans we craft for clients, we added a small piece in a three-year annuity, which could be annuitized in the future, adding another income stream for life. Due to his age, the payout for Mr. Johnson would be around 9% each year, lasting forever. If he waits to start the income stream, called annuitization, his payout percentage would increase due to a shorter life expectancy. For the meantime, the annuity will stay in deferral and grow at a guaranteed 4% per year. We are sacrificing return today to have the annuitization option in the future.

Within his IRA, we used half the money in an illiquid REIT and the other half in the liquid adaptive management account. Since he is required to pull out minimum distributions each year, we will use the managed account to satisfy this requirement, allowing the REIT to reinvest and grow.

Finally, when it came to the capital gains issue, he agreed with us that it was better to pay a little tax today and get the money working harder for him going forward, rather than sitting in on investment earning nothing year after year and continuing to defer the tax. By paying the tax, he was free to invest the proceeds into investments with a better probability of providing income and growth.

One point to remember: Tax considerations should always be secondary to the right investment choice. Time and time again, we've seen clients hold on to poor performing investments because they didn't want to realize any taxable gains. The losses on the investments ended up being far greater than any tax bill would have ever been.

Our recommendations for Mr. Johnson were as follows:

Original Position	Amount	Recommended Position	Amount	Asset Class	Liquidity Timeline
IRA	$50,000	⇒ Health Care REIT	$25,000	Institutional Grade Real Estate	4 Years
		Adaptive Asset Management	$25,000	Stock Market	Liquid

Original Position	Amount	Recommended Position	Amount	Asset Class	Liquidity Timeline
Stocks, Mutual Funds	$300,000	⇒ Storage Center REIT	$33,000	Institutional Grade Real Estate	4 Years
		Ultra Low LTV Office REIT	$33,000	Institutional Grade Real Estate	4 Years
		Single Tenant Big Box REIT	$34,000	Institutional Grade Real Estate	3 Years
		Fixed Annuity	$50,000	Insurance	3 Years
		Adaptive Asset Management	$150,000	Stock Market	Liquid

Summary of Recommendations for Mr. Johnson:

Fixed Annuity	$50,000	~ 13% of investable wealth
Non-Traded REITs	$125,000	~ 30%
Adaptive Asset Management	$175,000	~ 44%
CDs	$50,000	~ 13%

Summary of Liquid to Illiquid investments

Liquid Investments	$225,000	~ 56% of investable wealth
Illiquid Investments	$175,000	~ 44%

Liquidity Time Line	$ Becoming Liquid	Total Liquid Investments
Liquid Immediately	$225,000	$225,000
Liquid after 3 years	$84,000	$309,000
Liquid after 4 years	$91,000	$400,000

Mr. Johnson paid forty-five thousand dollars for his house, thirty years ago, and likes the idea of real estate as a major part of his plan, as it has earned him more money than any other investment he has ever owned. He believes rents will generally increase over time and will help offset his income needs with rising inflation. The four REITs chosen for him match his beliefs of what will hold its value over the coming years. The office REIT has a loan to value ratio of around 15%, and he felt that would provide adequate protection in a downturn, along with the other three choices.

Though the annuity will probably not perform as well as the non-traded REITS or the adaptive management account, 4% is better than current CD interest rates in the low 1–2% range. More importantly, he can annuitize the contract to begin a much higher payout for the rest of his life, currently around 9%. This again is due to his life expectancy, when calculating the payment percentage. The older you are the higher the percentage and vice versa.

We chose a short-term annuity, which we can change in just three years if the economic environment warrants it. The surrender charges on this particular annuity were 5%, 4%, and 3% and 0% after year three. If necessary, he could surrender the policy by day 366, or the beginning of year two, effectively give back the interest earned to date, and walk away with his original principal. Again, this is a worst-case scenario. If interest rates rise dramatically within the next three years, we will be able to close the annuity penalty free after year three and move the money to a harder working financial vehicle.

Finally, we left the fifty-thousand-dollar CD alone because this is an account that provides him piece of mind. That is always worth more than gaining an extra couple of percentage points by moving the money. Always design a plan around your beliefs, not somebody else's.

Ms. Jonas

Ms. Jonas is fifty-five years old and single. She does not work and lives off an inheritance she received from her deceased parents. She loves to travel and maintains a condo in a downtown high rise. The condo works nicely with her lifestyle, as it allows her the flexibility to leave town on a moment's notice.

A list of her assets includes:

Personal Residence	Fair Market Value (FMV) $1,000,000 and paid off
Muni Bonds	$2,300,000
Rental Property	FMV $800,000 with $100,000 in loans Cost basis of $300,000 Net Cash Flow of $18,000 per year
Net worth including Residence	$4,000,000

Investable wealth:

Muni Bonds	$2,300,000
Rental Property	$700,000 ($800,000 – Mortgage = $700,000)
Total	$3,000,000

Maximum per Real Asset financial investment:
Investable Wealth x 10% = $3,000,000 x 10% = $300,000

Though we are not fans of muni-bonds in this rising interest rate environment, Ms. Jonas' bonds were appropriate for her. Her current advisor had chosen an ultra short duration portfolio of individual bonds, with the longest maturation date a mere two years out. She had more income than she knew what to do with and was comfortable with the portfolio.

We recommended doing nothing with the bonds and instead focused our attention on her property. Discussing her rental property, she said it was the one nuisance in her life. The terrible T's (tenants, toilets, and trash) were driving her crazy. She felt tied to the property due to the capital gains she would owe when selling it. If she sold, she would realize five hundred thousand dollars in capital gains, and with the recapture of depreciation, her tax bill would be over one hundred twenty-five thousand dollars. The taxes paid would represent a huge leak in her financial bucket of lost opportunity.

We taught her about 1031 exchanges, (discussed in detail in Appendix B) and showed her options using Tenants-in-Common (TICS). These securities allow her to sell the property and do a 1031 exchange into multiple co-ownership real estate properties for maximum diversification and deferral of all the taxes.

Our recommendations for Ms. Jonas were as follows:

Original Position	Amount		Recommended Position	Amount	Asset Class	Liquidity Timeline
Rental Property	$700,000	⇨	Storage Center TIC	$200,000	Institutional Grade Real Estate	5~7 Years
		1031 tax deferred exchange	Single AAA Credit Tenant Office TIC	$200,000	Institutional Grade Real Estate	5~7 Years
			400 Unit Apartment Complex TIC	$200,000	Institutional Grade Real Estate	5~7 Years
			Oil Royalty	$100,000	Oil/Gas	? Years

The average target yield for the properties selected was around 7%. By exchanging the equity in one property into four distinctly different properties, she was able to diversify her holdings and raise her net cash flow from eighteen thousand to around fifty thousand dollars. The part that surprised her was how many large commercial properties can accelerate depreciation via a cost segregation study.

This study effectively identifies and reclassifies real estate assets into four categories: personal property, land improvements, building components, and land. The first three have accelerated depreciation deductions and easier write-offs when an asset becomes obsolete, broken, or destroyed. The net effect of using a cost segregation study for TICs in general is that, for Ms. Jonas' income of fifty thousand dollars, she may only have net taxable income of fifteen to twenty thousand dollars. Basically, the same situation she was in before the 1031 exchange. The other headache she was relieved of was that of tax reporting, which is essentially prepared by the sponsor of the TIC and mailed to the owners. The owners just hand the forms to their accountants and they are done.

There are trade-offs for TICs, the biggest one being a very limited ability to sell one's ownership share during the duration of the investment, typically between four to seven years. This wasn't a concern for Ms. Jonas, considering she had owned her property for over twenty years.

TICs require a lot of education concerning the pros and cons and should only be considered after careful due diligence and working with a financial advisor who spends a lot of time doing TIC investments. Other negative attributes are the same negative attributes that affect all real estate investments. Income can be suspended if the property loses tenants, additional cash requirements may be needed if significant issues arise with the property, and others.

Though Ms. Jonas didn't really care about the increase in income, she was thrilled to no longer have to deal with the Terrible T's. The TICs she purchased all came with professional management. Now, she is truly free to leave town without any of the headaches of managing a property and being on call to deal with them.

Mr. and Mrs. Jasper

Mr. Jasper is thirty-four years old, a graphic artist with income around forty-five thousand dollars per year. He is married and has an eighteen-month-old son named Grant. His wife, Mrs. Jasper, is thirty-three years old and works as a nurse part-time earning, thirty-six thousand dollars per year. Their son currently needs daycare two days per week. The family rents a two-bedroom apartment for one thousand dollars per month.

A list of their assets includes:

Mr. Jasper's 401(k)	$12,000
Mrs. Jasper's	$4,000
After tax Mutual Funds	$39,000
Net worth	$55,000

With a combined income of eighty-one thousand dollars per year and net worth of fifty-five thousand dollars, the Jaspers are considered non-accredited investors. In general, they need a high degree of liquidity for whatever comes their way, and tying up money in illiquid investments would not be prudent. The most appropriate advice we could give them was to shift their static mutual funds to an adaptive money manager with a lower net cost and superior performance over the past ten years, compared to their current static funds. They are still in the stock market but now will have a group truly managing their small nest egg.

Because the Jaspers are young with family liabilities, we also recommended term life policies for both spouses, due to their having similar incomes. Because of their ages, both applied for twenty-five-year term policies for $1 million each, with a cost of around six hundred dollars for him and four hundred dollars for her. Anytime a family has young children at home, life insurance becomes a necessity.

Does eighty-three dollars per month cut into the amount they could be saving? Of course it does, but it is a hedge against either or both of them being killed and leaving the other or their son Grant facing financial hardship. It is important to consider the loss of future income and costs associated with college or other typical expenses of raising a child. We recommended the twenty-five-year term policies to cover them past college years for Grant and to around age sixty for themselves. At that point, family liabilities tend to ease, but other liabilities, such as mortgage, job, estate and so forth, may deem a continued need for insurance or changing the coverage to a permanent policy.

The most important education we gave the Jaspers was to teach them to shift their focus from making only 401(k) contributions to saving up and eventually buying a small rental property and using their normal retirement contributions to cover their base rental costs (mortgage and property taxes). The adaptive money management account could be used for a down payment, if and when they decide to buy their first property. At our firm, we do not find properties for clients but only work as sounding boards if they have questions during the process, such as what type of mortgage would we recommend or how to find a good property manager. Our goal was to steer the Jaspers into real asset wealth and toward generating additional cash flow every month, a tried and true wealth building principle.

Many people would argue that we should have guided them into purchasing a home first. While this is desirable for many, we teach our clients to buy assets first, liabilities second. If successful, the Jaspers may eventually have enough cash flow coming from various small rental properties to equal a mortgage payment on their own house. Then they would be effectively mortgage-free!

Mr. Warbucks

Mr. Warbucks is sixty-seven years old, married, with lots of grandkids. He recently sold a patent to a big turbine manufacturer for $50 million. He had excellent tax and estate planning already in place and was looking for a financial advisor to guide him in placing the money. Needless to say, this client was shopping all the big names, and they all were putting on their best dog and pony shows for him.

This client came to us after seeing the proposals from the major wire houses and most of the boutique firms in the area. His comment to me was that the plans from everyone so far were pretty much the same: stocks and muni-bonds. They all discussed the need for lower taxes and the over emphasis on muni-bonds.

His concerns about the proposals presented:

- Interest rates were at the bottom and would put downside pressure on stocks and bonds.
- Income needs for himself and his family would always be going up with inflation, and he wanted a better hedge for the future.
- He wanted a lot of flexibility for the majority of his money within five years, due to the unpredictability of the economy.

Here is the plan presented to Mr. Warbucks:

Original Position	Amount	Recommended Position	Amount	Asset Class	Liquidity Timeline
CASH	$45,000,000 ⇨	Oil/Gas Royalty	$4,000,000	Oil/Gas Royalty	Generational
		Energy Drilling	$4,000,000	Oil/Gas Developmental Drilling	? Years
		TIC Single Owner- 5 Properties	$15,000,000	Institutional Grade Real Estate	5~7 Years
		Non-Traded REIT	$9,000,000	Institutional Grade Real Estate	3~4 Years
		Energy Bond	$5,000,000	Oil/Gas	3 Years
		30 Year Fixed Notes	$3,000,000	Collateralized Notes: 30% LTV	1 Year
		Muni Bonds	$5,000,000	Stock Market	Liquid

CASH	$5,000,000 ⇨	FUN MONEY ☺	$5,000,000	REWARD	Goal: Spend within one year

Alternate Idea: Replace some real estate with money management to provide more liquidity.

CASH	$5,000,000 ⇨	Adaptive Asset Management	$5,000,000	Stock Market	Liquid

Income Analysis:

Investment	Target Income Assumption	Investment Amount	Income Per Month	Income Per Year	Depreciation %
Oil/Gas Royalty	10%	$4,000,000	$33,333	$400,000	20%
Oil/Gas Drilling	15%	$4,000,000	$50,000	$600,000	20%
Real Estate – TICS	7%	$15,000,000	$87,500	$1,050,000	50%
Non-traded REITs	6.5%	$9,000,000	$48,750	$585,000	60%
Energy Bond	12%	$5,000,000	$50,000	$600,000	0%
Collateralized Notes	6%	$3,000,000	$15,000	$180,000	0%
Muni Bonds	5%	$5,000,000	$20,833	$250,000	0%
Average 8.14%		$45,000,000	$305,417	$3,665,000	

Approximate Taxable Income After Depreciation Deduction:	$2,339,000
After applying Energy Drilling tax deduction of $800,000 per year for five years.	-$800,000
Taxable Income Approximate:	$1,539,000

When looking through our plan, the first thing he noticed was the smiley face and fun money category. My comment to him was, "Congratulations, you just won a very well-deserved spending spree. Spend all the money in this category within a year. Blow it on every frivolous idea you can imagine, spend it on your kids, grandkids, the neighbors' grandkids, your favorite charity. Enjoy it. You worked very hard for this accomplishment." With a smile on his face, considering the spending possibilities, we got down to business.

After describing to him our philosophy on wealth and the use of numerous legs on one's financial table to provide stability and income, I broke down the individual pieces and how they related to the overall plan.

Starting with the real estate portion, we had a combination of single owner TICs, alongside non-traded REITS. The single owner TICs were meant for him to have total control over the buildings and the final say. There would be no other owners to cloud discussions about management, possible sell dates, etc. The money that went into these properties would grow effectively capital gains tax-free forever due to the planned use of 1031 exchanges whenever a building would be sold. As previously mentioned and further explained in Appendix B, when Mr. Warbucks passes away, those buildings will receive a step-up in cost basis, and the next generation will inherit them without any capital gain tax burden. Both the TICs and the non-traded REITs provide a high degree of current income tax sheltering via depreciation and other pass through tax advantages.

We used the non-traded REITs for a smaller but significant chunk of his money for the shear diversification among hundreds of institutional grade real estate properties across the country, and in various categories from multifamily, storage, big box store, to office and timber.

The plan consisted of three types of energy DPPs we commonly use for clients. The royalty and energy bonds would provide for fairly stable income streams we could plan around, and the royalty programs would also provide a high degree of inflationary income protection. The energy drilling was used for two purposes: the first being the possibility of very high income distributions, the second being the immense income deductions available from intangible and tangible drilling costs associated with these programs. One option someone has when investing in an energy drilling program is to amortize the purchase amount over five years and receive 100% income deductions without concern for Alternative Minimum Tax (AMT) holdbacks. By placing $4 million into various energy drilling programs and amortizing the intangible and tangible drilling costs over five years, Mr. Warbucks will receive eight hundred thousand ($4 million over five years) of income deductions each year until they are exhausted.

Mr. Warbucks lives very modestly for someone who is worth so much. He does not have liquidity needs he could possibly foresee beyond a million or so. We placed $5 million into muni-bonds and $3 million in the short-term notes for the just-in-case needs he might encounter. Better safe than sorry. Who knows, he might on a whim want to purchase a house for each of his grandkids.

You'll notice we put down target projections for the various investments. These are target projections he felt were reasonable but understood that nothing was guaranteed. Although we did not only use muni-bonds as did the other advisors, when adding all the projected dividends along with the tax benefits, Mr. Warbucks was looking at cash flow approaching over three hundred thousand dollars per month, with a total taxable income of approximately one third or one hundred thousand dollars per month. Though he will have to pay roughly half in taxes on the taxable portion, around fifty thousand dollars each month, it still leaves him with approximately two hundred-fifty thousand dollars each month after tax, or $3 million a year.

Dividing $3 million by the starting principal ($45 million) results in an after-tax distribution of approximately 6.7%. An income far higher than most muni-bond portfolios will come close to paying with one added advantage. There is the potential for growth of his principal in the rising interest rate environment he expects, something the bonds will not likely achieve.

Lastly, the plan for Mr. Warbucks included a significant amount of advanced estate planning, charitable gifting, and life insurance. For the scope of this book we are just focusing on the diversification of the assets and generation of cash flow.

Summary of Recommendations for Mr. Warbucks:

Oil/Gas Investments	$13,000,000	~ 29% of investable wealth
Non-Traded REITs & TICS	$24,000,000	~ 53%
Collateralized Notes	$3,000,000	~ 7%
Muni Bonds	$5,000,000	~ 11%

Summary of Liquid to Illiquid investments

| Liquid Investments | $5,000,000 | ~ 11% of investable wealth |
| Illiquid Investments | $40,000,000 | ~ 89% |

Liquidity Time Line	$ Becoming Liquid	Total Liquid Investments
Liquid Immediately	$5,000,000	$5,000,000
Liquid after 1 year	$3,000,000	$8,000,000
Liquid after 3~4 years	$14,000,000	$22,000,000
Liquid after 5–7 years	$15,000,000	$37,000,000
Oil/Gas Royalty Payment	$8,000,000 Never Liquid	$37,000,000

Please note that when we were dealing with larger amounts like this and with someone who lives on only a very small portion of the cash flow generated, we were free to tie up the majority of the principal in illiquid investments, as in Mr. Warbucks' case, only needing about four hundred thousand per year. The client was looking for stability and income, the primary goal of the High Return–Capital Preservation category. The trade off again was limited liquidity.

The first and last thing Mr. Warbucks said about the plan was the use of the fun money category. "Funny," he said, "you were the first advisor who looked beyond the money and thought of me and my family and how we could improve our lives."

I believe many of the grandkids now have new homes.

———

Appendix B
1031 Real Estate Exchanges

What is a Tax-Deferred Exchange?

In a typical transaction, the property owner is taxed on any gain realized from the sale. However, through a Section 1031 Exchange, the tax on the gain is deferred until some future date.

Section 1031 of the Internal Revenue Service Code provides that no gain or loss shall be recognized on the exchange of property held for productive use in a trade or business, or for investment. A tax-deferred exchange is a method by which a property owner trades one or more relinquished properties for one or more replacement properties of "like-kind," while deferring the payment of federal income taxes and some state taxes on the transaction.

The theory behind Section 1031 is that when a property owner has reinvested the sale proceeds into another property, the economic gain has not been realized in a way that generates funds to pay any tax. In other words, the taxpayer's investment is still the same, only the form has changed (e.g. vacant land exchanged for apartment building). Therefore, it would be unfair to force the taxpayer to pay tax on a "paper" gain.

The like-kind exchange under Section 1031 is tax-deferred, not tax-free. When the replacement property is ultimately sold (not as part of another exchange), the original deferred gain, plus any additional gain realized since the purchase of the replacement property, is subject to tax.

What are the Benefits of Exchanging Versus Selling?

- A Section 1031 exchange is one of the few techniques available to postpone or potentially eliminate taxes due on the sale of qualifying properties.
- By deferring the tax, you have more money available to invest in another property. In effect, you receive an interest-free loan from the federal government, in the amount you would have paid in taxes.
- Any gain from depreciation recapture is postponed.
- You can acquire and dispose of properties to reallocate your investment portfolio without paying tax on any gain.

What are the Different Types of Exchanges?

- Simultaneous Exchange: The exchange of the relinquished property for the replacement property occurs at the same time.
- Delayed Exchange: This is the most common type of exchange. A Delayed Exchange occurs when there is a time gap between the transfer of the Relinquished Property and the acquisition of the Replacement Property. A Delayed Exchange is subject to strict time limits, which are set forth in the Treasury Regulations.
- Build-to-Suit (Improvement or Construction) Exchange: This technique allows the taxpayer to build on or make improvements to the replacement property using the exchange proceeds.
- Reverse Exchange: A situation where the replacement property is acquired prior to transferring the relinquished property. The IRS has offered a safe harbor for reverse exchanges, as outlined in Rev. Proc. 2000-37, effective September 15, 2000. These transactions are sometimes referred to as "parking arrangements" and may also be structured in ways that are outside the safe harbor.
- Personal Property Exchange: Exchanges are not limited to real property. Personal property can also be exchanged for other personal property of like-kind or like-class.

What are the Requirements for a Valid Exchange?

- Qualifying Property - Certain types of property are specifically excluded from Section 1031 treatment: property held primarily for sale; inventories; stocks, bonds or notes; other securities or evidences of indebtedness; interests in a partnership; certificates of trusts or beneficial interest; and chooses in action. In general, if property is not specifically excluded, it can qualify for tax-deferred treatment.

- Proper Purpose - Both the relinquished property and replacement property must be held for productive use in a trade or business or for investment. Property acquired for immediate resale will not qualify. The taxpayer's personal residence will not qualify.

- Like Kind - Replacement property acquired in an exchange must be "like-kind" to the property being relinquished. All qualifying real property located in the United States is like-kind. Personal property that is relinquished must be either like-kind or like-class to the personal property that is acquired. Property located outside the United States is not like-kind to property located in the United States.

- Exchange Requirement - The relinquished property must be exchanged for other property, rather than sold for cash and using the proceeds to buy the replacement property. Most deferred exchanges are facilitated by Qualified Intermediaries, who assist the taxpayer in meeting the requirements of Section 1031.

What are the General Guidelines to Follow in Order for a Taxpayer to Defer All the Taxable Gain?

- The value of the replacement property must be equal to or greater than the value of the relinquished property.
- The equity in the replacement property must be equal to or greater than the equity in the relinquished property.
- The debt on the replacement property must be equal to or greater than the debt on the relinquished property.
- All of the net proceeds from the sale of the relinquished property must be used to acquire the replacement property.

When Can I Take Money Out of the Exchange Account?

Once the money is deposited into an exchange account, funds can only be withdrawn in accordance with the regulations. The taxpayer cannot receive any money until the exchange is complete. If you want to receive a portion of the proceeds in cash, this must be done before the funds are deposited with the Qualified Intermediary.

Can the Replacement Property Eventually Be Converted to the Taxpayer's Primary Residence or a Vacation Home?

Yes, but the holding requirements of Section 1031 must be met prior to changing the primary use of the property. The IRS has no specific regulations on holding periods. However, many experts feel that to be on the safe side, the taxpayer should hold the replacement property for a proper use for a period of at least one year.

If the owner later on wants to take advantage of the homeowner's exemption (up to two hundred-fifty thousand dollars or five hundred thousand dollars for a couple), there is now a five-year holding period requirement.

What is a Qualified Intermediary (QI)?

A Qualified Intermediary is an independent party who facilitates tax-deferred exchanges pursuant to Section 1031 of the Internal Revenue Code. The QI cannot be the taxpayer or a disqualified person.

- Acting under a written agreement with the taxpayer, the QI acquires the relinquished property and transfers it to the buyer.
- The QI holds the sales proceeds to prevent the taxpayer from having actual or constructive receipt of the funds.
- Finally, the QI acquires the replacement property and transfers it to the taxpayer to complete the exchange within the appropriate time limits.

Why is a Qualified Intermediary Needed?

The exchange ends the moment the taxpayer has actual or constructive receipt (i.e. direct or indirect use or control) of the proceeds from the sale of the relinquished property. The use of a QI is a safe harbor established by the Treasury Regulations. If the taxpayer meets the requirements of this safe harbor, the IRS will not consider the taxpayer to be in receipt of the funds. The sale proceeds go directly to the QI, who holds them until they are needed to acquire the replacement property. The QI then delivers the funds directly to the closing agent.

Can the Taxpayer Just Sell the Relinquished Property and Put the Money in a Separate Bank Account, Only to Be Used for the Purchase of the Replacement Property?

The IRS regulations are very clear. The taxpayer may not receive the proceeds or take constructive receipt of the funds in any way, without disqualifying the exchange.

If the Taxpayer has Already Signed a Contract to Sell the Relinquished Property, is it Too Late to Start a Tax-Deferred Exchange?

No, as long as the taxpayer has not transferred title or the benefits and burdens of the relinquished property, she can still set up a tax-deferred exchange. Once the closing occurs, it is too late to take advantage of a Section 1031 tax-deferred exchange, even if the taxpayer has not cashed the proceeds check.

Does the Qualified Intermediary Actually Take Title to the Properties?

No, not in most situations. The IRS regulations allow the properties to be deeded directly between the parties, just as in a normal sale transaction. The taxpayer's interests in the property purchase and sale contracts are assigned to the QI. The QI then instructs the property owner to deed the property directly to the appropriate party (for the relinquished property, its buyer, and for the replacement property, taxpayer).

What are the Time Restrictions on Completing a Section 1031 Exchange?

A taxpayer has forty-five days after the date that the relinquished property is transferred to properly identify potential replacement properties. The exchange must be completed by the date that is 180 days after the transfer of the relinquished property, or the due date of the taxpayer's federal tax return for the year in which the relinquished property was transferred, whichever is earlier. Thus, for a calendar year taxpayer, the exchange period may be cut short for any exchange that begins after October 17th. However, the taxpayer can get the full 180 days by obtaining an extension of the due date for filing the tax return.

What if the Taxpayer Cannot Identify any Replacement Property Within Forty-Five Days or Close on a Replacement Property Before the End of the Exchange Period?

Unfortunately, there are no extensions available. If the taxpayer does not meet the time limits, the exchange will fail, and the taxpayer will have to pay any taxes arising from the sale of the relinquished property, *unless the IRS has expressly granted extensions in specified disaster area(s).*

Is there any Limit to the Number of Properties that Can be Identified?

There are three rules that limit the number of properties that can be identified. The taxpayer must meet the requirements of at least one of these rules:

- Three-Property Rule: The taxpayer may identify up to three potential replacement properties, without regard to their value; or
- 200% Rule: Any number of properties may be identified, but their total value cannot exceed twice the value of the relinquished property, or
- 95% Rule: The taxpayer may identify as many properties as he wants, but before the end of the exchange period, the taxpayer must acquire replacement properties with an aggregate fair market value equal to at least 95% of the aggregate fair market value of all the identified properties.

What are the Requirements to Properly Identify Replacement Property?

Potential replacement property must be identified in writing, signed by the taxpayer, and delivered to a party to the exchange who is not considered a "disqualified person." A "disqualified" person is anyone who has a relationship with the taxpayer that is so close that the person is presumed to be under the control of the taxpayer. Examples include blood relatives, and any person who is or has been the taxpayer's attorney, accountant, investment banker, or real estate agent within the two years prior to the closing of the relinquished property. The identification cannot be made orally.

Are Section 1031 Exchanges Limited only to Real Estate?

No. Any property that is held for productive use in a trade or business, or for investment, may qualify for tax-deferred treatment under Section 1031. In fact, many exchanges are "multi-asset" exchanges, involving both real property and personal property.

What is a "Multi-Asset" Exchange?

A multi-asset exchange involves both real and personal property. For example, the sale of a hotel will typically include the underlying land and buildings, as well as the furnishings and equipment. If the taxpayer wants to exchange the hotel for a similar property, he would exchange the land and buildings as one part of the exchange. The furnishings and equipment would be separated into groups of like-kind or like-class property, with the groups of relinquished property being exchanged for groups of replacement property.

Although the definition of like-kind is much narrower for personal property and business equipment, careful planning will allow the taxpayer to enjoy the benefits of an exchange for the entire relinquished property, not just for the real estate portion.

What is a Reverse Exchange?

A reverse exchange, sometimes called a "parking arrangement," occurs when a taxpayer acquires a Replacement Property before disposing of their Relinquished Property. A "pure" reverse exchange, where the taxpayer owns both the Relinquished and Replacement properties at the same time, is not allowed. The actual acquisition of the "parked" property is done by an Exchange Accommodation Titleholder (EAT) or parking entity.

Is a Reverse Exchange Permissible?

Yes. Although the Treasury Regulations still do not apply to reverse exchanges, the IRS issued "safe harbor" guidelines for reverse exchanges on September 15, 2000, in Revenue Procedure 2000-37. Compliance with the safe harbor creates certain presumptions that will enable the transaction to qualify for Section 1031 tax-deferred exchange treatment.

How Does a Reverse Exchange Work?

In a typical reverse (or "parking") exchange, the "Exchange Accommodation Titleholder" (EAT) takes title to ("parks") the replacement property and holds it until the taxpayer is able to sell the relinquished property. The taxpayer then exchanges with the EAT, who now owns the replacement property. An exchange structured within the safe harbor of Rev. Proc. 2000-37 cannot have a parking period that goes beyond 180 days.

What Happens if the Exchange Cannot be Completed Within 180 days?

If the reverse exchange period exceeds 180 days, then the exchange is outside the safe harbor of Rev. Proc. 2000-37. With careful planning, it is possible to structure a reverse exchange that will go beyond 180 days, but the taxpayer will lose the presumptions that accompany compliance with the safe harbor.

Can the Proceeds from the Relinquished Property be Used to Make Improvements to the Replacement Property?

Yes. This is known as a Build-to-Suit or Construction or Improvement Exchange. It is similar in concept to a reverse exchange. The taxpayer is not permitted to build on property she already owns. Therefore, an unrelated party or parking entity must take title to the replacement property, make the improvements, and convey title to the taxpayer before the end of the exchange period.

What is the Difference Between "Realized" Gain and "Recognized" Gain?

Realized gain is the increase in the taxpayer's economic position as a result of the exchange. In a sale, tax is paid on the realized gain. Recognized gain is the taxable gain. Recognized gain is the lesser of realized gain or the net boot received.

What is Boot?

Boot is any property received by the taxpayer in the exchange that is not like-kind to the relinquished property. Boot is characterized as either "cash" boot or "mortgage" boot. Realized Gain is recognized to the extent of net boot received.

What is Mortgage Boot?
Mortgage Boot consists of liabilities assumed or given up by the taxpayer. The taxpayer pays mortgage boot when he assumes or places debt on the replacement property. The taxpayer receives mortgage boot when he is relieved of debt on the replacement property. If the taxpayer does not acquire debt that is equal to or greater than the debt that was paid off, they are considered to be relieved of debt. The debt relief portion is taxable, unless offset when netted against other boot in the transaction.

What is Cash Boot?
Cash Boot is any boot received by the taxpayer, other than mortgage boot. Cash boot may be in the form of money or other property.

What are the Boot "Netting" Rules?
- Cash boot paid offsets cash boot received
- Cash boot paid offsets mortgage boot received (debt relief)
- Mortgage boot paid (debt assumed) offsets mortgage boot received
- Mortgage boot paid does not offset cash boot received

I Bought the Property as a Single Person, and I Would Like to Acquire the Replacement Property Together with My Spouse.
The most conservative way is to stay consistent and complete the exchange the same way it was started and to add the spouse after the completion of the exchange. An exception can be made if there is a lender requirement that the spouse has to be added in order to qualify for a loan. If an exchange is planned well ahead of time, another solution would be to add the spouse to the title of the currently held property. Timing should be discussed with the CPA.

I Closed Escrow on My First Replacement Property Within the Forty-Five-Day Identification Period. Can I Now Identify Three More Properties Within My Forty-Five-Day Identification Period?
If you are using the three-property rule, the completed acquisition counts as one and you may identify only up to two additional properties.

How do I Identify Two Different Properties (or Percentages of Ownership Through a TIC) Covered by ONE Purchase Contract?
If the properties could be sold separately at a later date, they should be identified as two properties.

———

Index

Made in the USA
Charleston, SC
31 March 2010